Caring for a cat with hyperthyroidism

by Dr Sarah Caney

Published by Cat Professional Ltd

Copyright © Cat Professional Ltd 2009

www.catprofessional.com

ISBN 978-0-9556913-4-8

About Cat Professional

Cat Professional was founded in 2007 by Dr Sarah Caney with the aims of providing cat owners and veterinary professionals with the highest quality information, advice, training and consultancy services.

Publications

Cat Professional is a leading provider of high quality publications on caring for cats with a variety of medical conditions. Written by international experts in their field, each book is written to be understood by cat owners and veterinary professionals. The books are available to buy through the website www.catprofessional.com as eBooks where they can be downloaded and read instantly. Alternatively they can be purchased as a softback via the website and specialist bookstores.

'Caring for a cat with hyperthyroidism' is the fourth in a series of books published by Cat Professional. It adds to 'Caring for a cat with kidney failure' (published January 2008), 'Caring for a blind cat' (published August 2008) and 'Caring for a cat with lower urinary tract disease' (published January 2009). Forthcoming publications include 'Caring for a cat with diabetes mellitus', 'Caring for a geriatric cat', 'Caring for a cat with chronic gingivostomatitis' and 'Caring for a cat suffering from obesity'.

German and Japanese translations of each book will be made available.

A variety of free-to-download articles also feature on the Cat Professional website.

* All data is retained by Cat Professional and we do not share any sensitive information, such as names and contact details, with third parties.

Education

Cat Professional is dedicated to improving the standards of cat care and in this capacity is a provider of Continuing Professional Development to veterinary surgeons and other professionals working with cats around the world. Cat Professional also works closely with leading providers of cat products and foods providing training programmes, assisting with product literature and advising on product design and marketing.

Free to download articles and technical documents of interest to cat owners and veterinary professionals are available on the website.

Specialist feline medicine advice is available to veterinary professionals and cat owners world-wide. Details are available on the website.

Clinics and Research

Cat Professional runs Specialist Geriatric Clinics at the Dick Vet School, Edinburgh. Clinical trials are conducted via cat owners attending these clinics and via owner submitted questionnaires completed online. Owners of cats from around the world have registered their cats and are participating in these studies.

There are ongoing studies into feline kidney disease, lower urinary tract disease and hyperthyroidism. The results of the research will be published so that future generations of vets, cat owners and most importantly cats can benefit from the increased knowledge gained. If you would like to register your cat* for one or more of these studies please visit www.catprofessional.com/clinics.html

About the author

Sarah Caney (pictured right) is an internationally recognised veterinary specialist in feline medicine who has worked as a feline-only vet since 1994. She trained as a specialist at the University of Bristol, England and is one of only eight recognised specialists in feline medicine working within the UK. Sarah has written many articles for veterinarians and cat owners and works very closely with the UK cat charity, the Feline Advisory Bureau, FAB (www.fabcats.org). Sarah has written three books: 'Caring for a cat with kidney failure' and 'Caring for a cat with lower urinary tract disease' (the latter co-authored with Professor Danièlle Gunn-Moore) published by Cat Professional and 'Self-Assessment Colour Review of Feline Medicine' with another feline expert, Andy Sparkes (published by Manson). As a clinician she enjoys seeing a mixture of first opinion and referral feline patients. She has been invited to lecture on feline medicine at veterinary conferences all over the world. Sarah lives in Scotland and has a very handsome, elderly tabby cat called Hobi (pictured right).

About this book

This book has been written as an electronic book available for downloading or printing on demand. If you have obtained this book free from a friend or another source I would encourage you to visit my website www.catprofessional.com to obtain a bona fide copy of your own.

Words in green are contained in the glossary section at the end of the book.

Dedications and acknowledgements

I would like to dedicate this book to my husband Brendan and our children Sophie and 'Tarquinetta' (the bump!) for all of their love and support whilst I have been writing this book.

Thanks go to all of those colleagues, clients and friends for their advice on what should be included and, of course, to the cats pictured for all looking so gorgeous!

The pictures included in this book are the copyright of the author with the exception of:

- 'Shortcake', the hypothyroid kitten shown on page 52, included with the kind permission of Professor Tim Gruffydd-Jones, University of Bristol, UK.
- Pictures of the Wilkinson cats shown on pages 66-68 included with the kind permission of their owner Kathy and professional cat photographer Robert Fox (www.photopaws.co.uk).

CONTENTS

INTRODUCTION/FOREWORD 6

SECTION 1 | the emotional side of things 7

Receiving the news: coping with the emotional side of receiving a diagnosis of hyperthyroidism 7

SECTION 2 | explaining the science of hyperthyroidism 11

What is hyperthyroidism? 11
What effect do thyroid hormones have on the body? 11
What is the thyroid gland and what does a healthy thyroid gland do? 11
What causes hyperthyroidism? 12
Which cats most commonly suffer from hyperthyroidism? 13
Can hyperthyroidism be prevented? 13
What are the signs of hyperthyroidism? 13
Are there other illnesses which can mimic hyperthyroidism? 16
How is hyperthyroidism diagnosed? 17
What other tests are helpful in cats with hyperthyroidism? ... 27
What does treatment of a hyperthyroid cat involve? 32
How is hyperthyroidism treated? 33
Medical treatment of hyperthyroidism 35
What is the best way to medicate my cat? 41
Surgical treatment of hyperthyroidism 43
What is post-operative hypoparathyroidism? 46
Radioiodine treatment of hyperthyroidism 47
Other treatments for hyperthyroidism 49
What is hypothyroidism? 50
What is the best treatment for my hyperthyroid cat? 53
Can hyperthyroid cats with chronic kidney disease still receive treatment? 54
Can hyperthyroid cats with diabetes mellitus still receive treatment? 54

What about cats with thyroid carcinomas? 55
How can I give my cat the best quality and length of life possible? 56
Check-ups for hyperthyroid cats receiving medical treatment 56
Check-ups for hyperthyroid cats that have had surgical treatment or radioiodine 60
Are routine vaccinations and worming still needed in cats with hyperthyroidism? 63
What is the prognosis (long-term outlook) for cats with hyperthyroidism? 64

SECTION 3 | case illustrations 65

SECTION 4 | discussing your cat's health with your vet 69

SECTION 5 | further information 71

Knowing when to say 'goodbye' 71
Will I know when it's time to say goodbye to my cat and let him/her go? 71
What does euthanasia involve? 72
What happens to my cat's body after they die or are euthanased (put to sleep)? 72
How to cope with losing your cat 73
What about my other cat/s – are they likely to grieve? 74

Useful websites 75

Glossary of terms used by vets 78

Converting SI units to Conventional units and vice versa ... 86

INTRODUCTION/FOREWORD

Hyperthyroidism is considered to be a relatively 'new' illness since it was first diagnosed in 1979 in the United States. Since this time, the frequency of this diagnosis has increased with one recent study suggesting that 12% of the UK cat population over the age of nine years are diagnosed with this condition each year. Similar results have been reported in Australia, Germany, Japan and the United States. A recent publication reported that the frequency of hyperthyroidism in US cats is increasing and many UK vets also feel that this illness is becoming more common. This might be because of increased awareness of the disease (and hence it is being tested for more often) but could also be a result of the increasing life-length of many cats. Since we still do not fully understand the cause of hyperthyroidism, it is also possible that the disease is becoming more common for other reasons. Worldwide, hyperthyroidism is believed to be the most common hormonal disease in cats with diabetes mellitus ('sugar diabetes') a close second. The frequency of hyperthyroidism varies quite markedly according to where the cat lives – for example it is a common diagnosis in the US and UK but rarely diagnosed in Greece and Scandinavian countries.

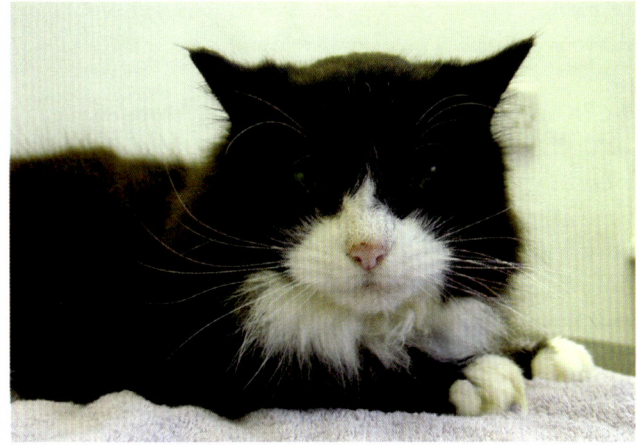

This guide has been written to provide cat owners with the information they need to understand this complex condition and provide the best care for their cat. The author regularly lectures on this subject and the contents of this book reflect what she teaches to veterinary students, veterinary nurses, technicians and qualified veterinary surgeons around the world.

Important Legal Information:

Cat Professional Ltd has developed this book with reasonable skill and care to provide general information on feline health and care in relation to feline hyperthyroidism. This book however does not, and cannot, provide advice on any individual situation. It is not a substitute for advice from a veterinary surgeon on each individual situation.

Cat Professional Ltd therefore strongly recommends that users seek, and follow, advice from their veterinary surgeon on any health or other care concerns that they may have concerning their cats. Users should not take, or omit to take, action concerning the health or care of their cats in reliance on the information contained in this book and so far as permissible by law, Cat Professional Ltd excludes all liability and responsibility for the consequences of any such action or omission in reliance on that information. While this book does not provide advice on, or recommend treatments or medications for, individual situations, users attention is brought to the fact that some of the medications referred to in this book may not be licensed (veterinary approved) in all countries and therefore may not be available in all countries.

SECTION 1 | the emotional side of things

Receiving the news: coping with the emotional side of receiving a diagnosis of hyperthyroidism

Being told that your cat has hyperthyroidism may have caused you some concern. Hyperthyroidism is a complicated condition to understand. This section will aim to reassure you as well as prepare you for what is to come.

What is wrong with my cat?

Hyperthyroidism is the veterinary term used to describe an illness resulting from having excessively high blood levels of thyroid hormones. All cats have a thyroid gland composed of two portions (referred to as thyroid 'lobes') in their neck. The thyroid hormones are required in healthy cats for many functions including normal growth and development and maintenance of a normal metabolic rate. Excessive blood levels of thyroid hormones (such as is the case with hyperthyroidism) are damaging to the body and ultimately this is a fatal illness if not treated.

Section 2 covers the scientific aspects of this condition in much greater detail – you can read about what we know about the causes of this condition, how vets diagnose hyperthyroidism and how it can best be treated. The good news is that this is considered to be a treatable condition – many cats can be cured of their clinical signs with appropriate treatment.

Could I have prevented this from happening – was it my fault?

Many people will immediately panic, thinking that they could have done more to prevent an illness from developing or that, if only they had taken their cat to the vet sooner, things might be different. Although it is impossible to generalise or comment specifically on an individual cat's circumstances, it is worth remembering that:

- Hyperthyroidism is not caused by anything that you as an owner or care provider have done.

- Although this is a condition which will get progressively worse with time, in most situations a short delay is unlikely to have changed your cat's chance of recovery.

SECTION 1 | the emotional side of things

What is the treatment for this disease?
There are three main treatment options for hyperthyroid cats:

- Medical treatment: prescribing antithyroid drugs which block production of thyroid hormones

- Surgical treatment: removal of the diseased thyroid tissue

- Radioiodine treatment: also referred to as radioactive iodine therapy, this is a form of radiotherapy that is able to treat abnormal thyroid tissue

Some hyperthyroid cats need additional medication for complications associated with their hyperthyroidism. For example, high blood pressure (systemic hypertension) is seen in a significant proportion of hyperthyroid cats and requires specific treatment.

Since hyperthyroidism is a condition which is common in older cats, it is not unusual for them to have more than one medical problem. Other common illnesses in older cats include a decline in kidney function (chronic kidney disease) and diabetes mellitus ('sugar diabetes'). If present, these conditions also require treatment.

All of the treatments are discussed in more detail in Section 2.

Is my cat in pain?
Hyperthyroidism is not believed to be a painful condition although some of the symptoms of illness can be distressing to a cat. For example, breathlessness, palpitations, irritability and anxiety can be seen with this condition.

Is it fair to put my cat on medication – am I being cruel to treat it?
Hyperthyroidism is considered to be a very treatable condition and it is possible to cure the illness in many cases. Not all cats require long-term medication, as this depends on which of the treatments is prescribed and whether the cat has other illnesses requiring therapy.

In many hyperthyroid cats, however, successful treatment involves long-term courses of medication. If your cat has been prescribed medication and you are concerned about how you may be able to give this to your cat, then it may be helpful to hear that:

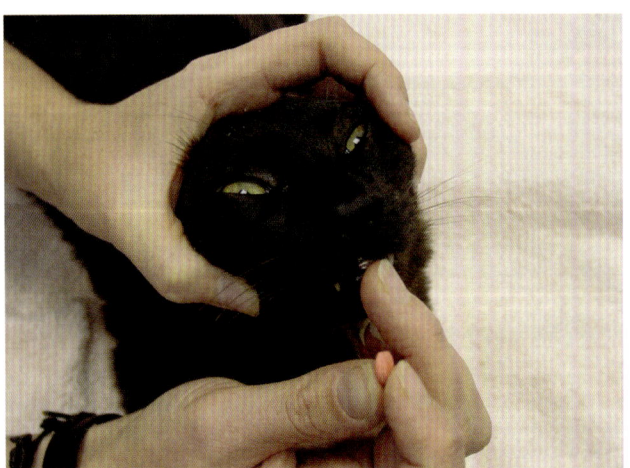

Left: Some cats are very easy to medicate with pills or capsules.

SECTION 1 | the emotional side of things

- Some cats are surprisingly easy to medicate.

- Some cats will eat treatments reliably in their food.

- In some countries, transdermal treatments are available for hyperthyroidism. These come as a skin cream which is usually applied to the inside of the cat's ear (a hairless area). The medication is absorbed through the skin and into the blood stream.

- For those cats on multiple medications empty gelatine capsules obtained from a vet or pharmacist can be very helpful. Several medicines can be put into one empty gelatine capsule reducing medication into one easy dosage.

- Advice on how to administer pills to a cat is contained on pages 41-43 and a link to a video showing how to give a pill to a cat is listed in the 'Useful websites' section.

It may take some time for you, and your cat, to get used to the treatment your vet has suggested but as long as your cat is happy and coping, it is worthwhile persevering. Don't forget to discuss how treatment is going with your vet – if you are having problems, they may well have solutions or suggestions for you.

Also, remember that we are talking about your cat – no one knows your cat better than you and if you feel that the treatment suggested is not right, for whatever reason, then your vet should respect this.

> **Hyperthyroidism is a treatable condition – many cats can be cured with appropriate therapy**

I'm not sure I can cope with treating my cat – help!
Learning of a diagnosis of hyperthyroidism may have come as a shock and will take some time to get used to. Once you have had a chance to think things through, chat with friends/family and your vet, hopefully everything will seem clearer and less daunting.

You can only do your best when it comes to caring for your cat and it is not always possible to do everything you want. For example if you have severe arthritis and are unable to give your cat a pill this may affect the level of treatment you can provide. Likewise, if your cat is completely intolerant to the thought of being medicated, this may prevent you from giving some treatments to it. In many situations, there are other options available – for example trying to hide medications in food or considering treatments which do not involve daily medications such as surgery or radioiodine. In any case, your vet should be able to talk you through the options and, together, you should be able to make a plan that you both feel comfortable with. The treatments for hyperthyroidism are discussed in more detail in Section 2.

SECTION 1 | the emotional side of things

Is hyperthyroidism life-threatening?
If left untreated, hyperthyroidism will eventually result in death as this illness has serious consequences on internal organs such as the heart. With appropriate treatment it is considered to be an illness which can be controlled and often cured.

This is discussed in more detail in Section 2.

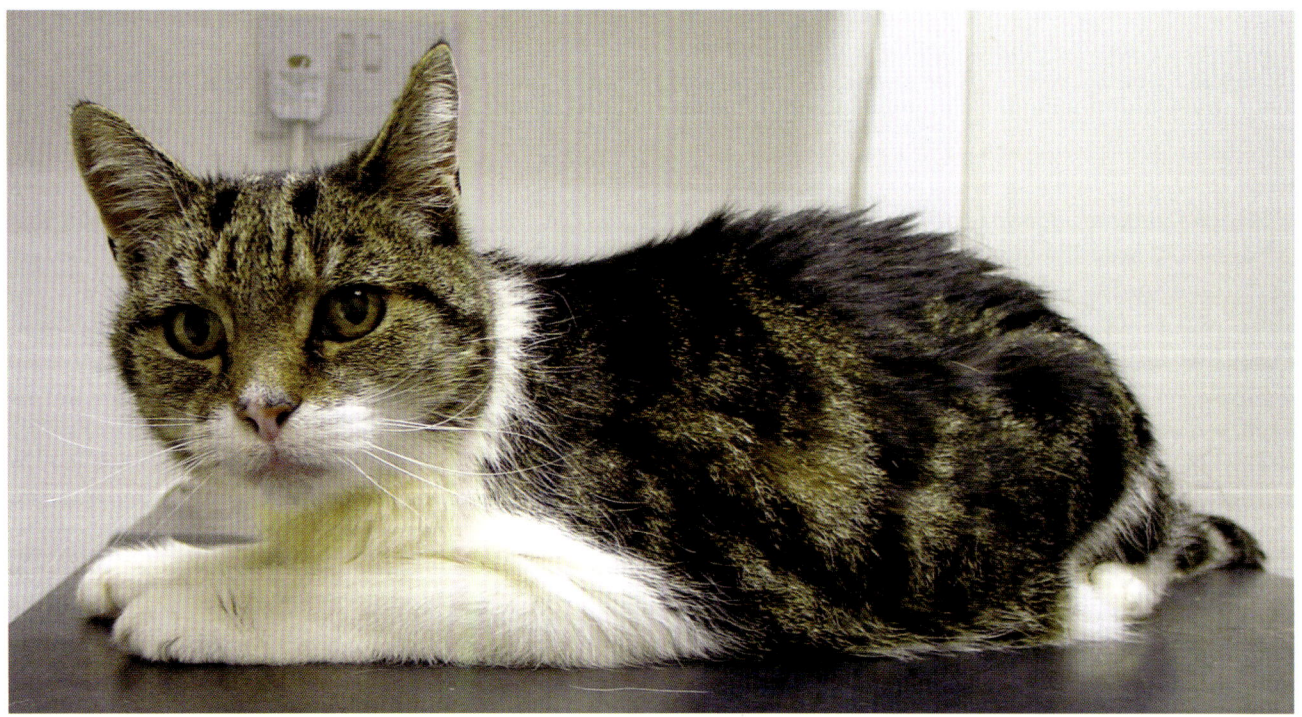

SECTION 2 | explaining the science of hyperthyroidism

What is hyperthyroidism?

Hyperthyroidism is the medical term for a situation where there are excessive blood levels of thyroid hormones. Some clinicians call this condition thyrotoxicosis. Thyroid hormones are produced by the thyroid gland. There are two thyroid hormones – T3 (triiodothyronine) and T4 (thyroxine).

What effect do thyroid hormones have on the body?

Thyroid hormones act on most body cells and in general their effects are to:

- increase the metabolic rate

- increase the heart rate (number of heart beats per minute) and the force of each heart beat

- increase blood pressure

- increase gastrointestinal (bowel) movement which can cause diarrhoea and/ vomiting

- increase activity levels – affected cats can be very restless and hyperactive

- reduce bodyweight (i.e. cause weight loss)

- reduce the amount of time the cat spends asleep

- aid in control of body temperature (thermoregulation)

What is the thyroid gland and what does a healthy thyroid gland do?

The thyroid gland is normally located in the cat's neck, just below the larynx (voice box). The thyroid gland is made up of two lobes – one on each side of the body. Some cats also have 'ectopic' (sometimes clinicians use the term 'accessory') thyroid tissue. Ectopic is the medical term for tissue at an unusual location. Ectopic thyroid tissue can be found under the tongue, in the neck and, most commonly, in the chest cavity.

Iodine present in the diet is absorbed into the circulation where it is taken to the thyroid gland. Iodine is actively concentrated in the thyroid where it is used to make the thyroid hormones, T3 and T4. Both of these hormones are released into the circulation from where they can act on all of the cells of the body. Thyroid hormones are required to regulate the body's metabolism. Production and release of thyroid hormones is under tight control in healthy cats. The hormone TRH (thyrotropin releasing hormone, produced in a part of the brain called the hypothalamus) stimulates production of TSH (thyrotropin or thyroid stimulating hormone, produced in a part of the brain called the pituitary) which in turn stimulates production and release of the thyroid hormones. Presence of T4 and T3 inhibits production of TRH and TSH so that levels

SECTION 2 | explaining the science of hyperthyroidism

of these thyroid hormones remain within a healthy balance. In hyperthyroid cats, the thyroid gland 'ignores' TSH and works autonomously (under its own control). The end result of this is abnormally high blood levels of thyroid hormones which causes a range of problems, as discussed later.

What causes hyperthyroidism?

There is still much not known about the cause of hyperthyroidism. This is a relatively new illness (first diagnosed in the United States in 1979) which varies in frequency around the world and even within individual countries. These findings have led to theories that genetic, dietary and/or environmental factors might be to blame for the disease. The belief that feline genetics may play a role in the development of hyperthyroidism is supported by the fact that one study showed that Siamese and Himalayan breed cats were ten times *less* likely to suffer from hyperthyroidism than the rest of the cat population.

Siamese cats are believed to be less vulnerable to developing hyperthyroidism than other cats.

Several studies have been done to try and identify common environmental factors which may be involved in causing hyperthyroidism. A recent publication looked at brominated flame retardants (PBDEs: commonly used in soft furnishings and electronic equipment) as these substances have been reported to alter thyroid function in other species. Although older cats tended to have higher levels of these substances than younger cats, no significant association was found between hyperthyroidism and levels of PBDEs. Other studies have looked at nutritional factors such as the iodine content of diets and tried to assess whether this is a factor in development of the disease. 'Risk factors' – factors increasing the chance that a cat will suffer from hyperthyroidism – have been identified in some studies although much of this data is controversial. For example some studies have shown that eating a wet diet (for example canned foods), having an indoor lifestyle and regular use of flea sprays increases the risk of hyperthyroidism. However, some of these factors are probably more associated with increasing life length of the cat (and hence increasing its chances of developing an illness common in older cats) rather than specific causes

SECTION 2 | explaining the science of hyperthyroidism

of hyperthyroidism. At this stage no specific cause has been identified and concerns over hyperthyroidism would not be a good reason to change from a wet to a dry catfood for example.

In the majority of cases, estimated to be 98% or more, hyperthyroidism is caused by a benign overgrowth of the thyroid tissue. This is sometimes referred to as a thyroid adenoma or adenomatous hyperplasia. In less than 2% of cases, hyperthyroidism is caused by a malignant growth (cancer) called a thyroid carcinoma or adenocarcinoma. Thyroid carcinomas are much more serious and need very different treatment from 'routine' hyperthyroid cases. Thyroid carcinomas are discussed in more detail on page 55.

In most cats (estimated >70%), hyperthyroidism is a bilateral condition – in other words, both lobes of the thyroid are affected by the disease. In the remainder of cats, the hyperthyroidism only affects one lobe and so is called unilateral. Some of these cases go on to develop bilateral disease at a later stage in their life.

Which cats most commonly suffer from hyperthyroidism?

Hyperthyroidism is most common in older cats – the most common age group being diagnosed are 10 to 13 years. It is unusual to diagnose hyperthyroidism is cats under seven years of age – less than 5% of cases are diagnosed in this age group. However, this condition has been reported in a few very young cats (the youngest being eight months) although this is very rare. Male and female cats appear to be affected with equal frequency.

Can hyperthyroidism be prevented?

Since the cause of hyperthyroidism has not been identified, at the moment there is little that can be done to prevent this condition. Until we understand the cause of this illness there is no prevention programme that can be recommended.

What are the signs of hyperthyroidism?

The clinical signs of hyperthyroidism vary in severity. Clinical signs are most severe in those cats that have been suffering with the illness for longer and in those that have additional (also referred to as 'concurrent') illnesses. Chronic kidney disease is one of the most common concurrent illnesses and this results in a worsening of many of the clinical signs.

Clinical signs of hyperthyroidism that an owner may notice commonly include:

- Weight loss

- An increased hunger and often insatiable appetite (referred to as polyphagia)

- Hyperactivity, anxiety/nervousness and restlessness

SECTION 2 | explaining the science of hyperthyroidism

Weight loss is a common clinical sign associated with hyperthyroidism and can be dramatic.

A small number of hyperthyroid cats are breathless and/or breathe with their mouth open. Many of these cats are suffering from heart disease as a consequence of their hyperthyroidism.

- An increased thirst (polydipsia) and increased amount of urine produced (polyuria)

- Diarrhoea and/or vomiting

- Poor coat and skin condition, for example matted, greasy and generally unkempt

Less common clinical signs of hyperthyroidism include:

- Laboured breathing, breathlessness and panting (breathing with the mouth open)

- Weakness, depression and lethargy

- Voice changes

- Reduced or variable appetite

- Heat intolerance – seeking out cool places to sleep

Cats showing depression, lethargy and reduced appetite are often referred to as 'apathetic' hyperthyroid cases. Some of these cats are even overweight rather than thin. Apathetic means that the cat appears indifferent, showing no emotion or animation.

SECTION 2 | explaining the science of hyperthyroidism

Most apathetic hyperthyroid cats are suffering from severe heart abnormalities associated with their hyperthyroidism.

A veterinary clinical examination may find the following additional abnormalities in a hyperthyroid cat:

- An enlarged thyroid gland that can be felt (the technical term for this is 'palpated') by the vet. An enlarged thyroid is referred to as a 'goitre' or thyroid nodule (a nodule is a lump). The goitre is usually palpated in the neck, just below the larynx (voice box), on one or both sides of the trachea (wind pipe). The size of the goitre can vary enormously. In most cases the goitre is not visible by eye and is the size of a garden pea. In rare cases the goitre can be as large as a golf ball. The goitre is usually mobile to a certain degree – in other words it is possible to move it by a few millimetres under the surface of the skin. In most patients, both thyroid lobes are enlarged ('bilateral' thyroid disease). In some cats, more than two areas of enlarged thyroid can be felt due to disease of normal and ectopic thyroid tissue.

In a small number of cats, the enlarged thyroid cannot be felt. This may be for several reasons:

– The cat may be tense and difficult to examine: it is easiest to feel a thyroid nodule (lump) when the cat is relaxed.

– The thyroid is so enlarged and heavy that it has descended, with gravity, into the chest cavity. Sometimes, 'tipping' the cat gently (holding the back legs up while the cat stands with their forelimb paws on the examination table) can

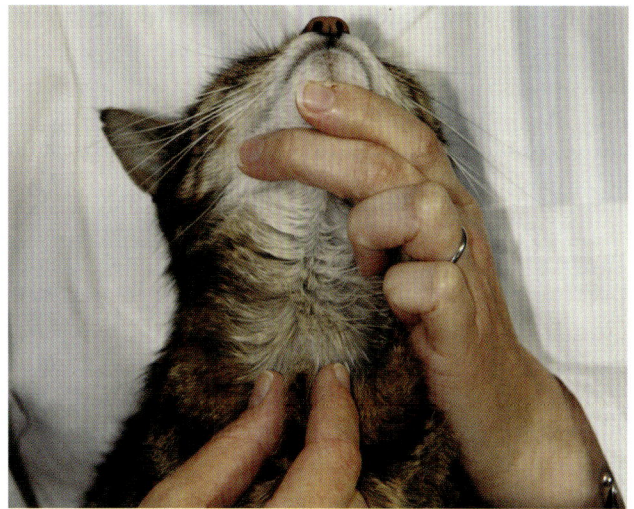

In most hyperthyroid cats, the goitre can be felt.

allow the goitre to be felt at the bottom of the neck.

– Although the thyroid is producing too much hormone, it is not very large and so difficult to feel.

– The diseased thyroid tissue is ectopic – in an abnormal location. Most commonly, ectopic thyroid tissue is located in the chest cavity and hence cannot be felt by a vet. Although the exact frequency of ectopic hyperthyroidism is not known, published reports suggest that up to as many as 20% of hyperthyroid cats may have this condition. Many cats with ectopic hyperthyroid tissue also have a palpable goitre.

SECTION 2 | explaining the science of hyperthyroidism

In the very small number of cats with malignant thyroid carcinomas, a type of cancer, the thyroid may feel stuck to underlying tissues and/or the skin. In some of these cases, the thyroid may feel more like an area of thickening rather than a specific lump. There may also be some enlargement of lymph glands (lymph nodes) in the same area due to spread of the cancer.

Occasionally cats will have a goitre but not be suffering from hyperthyroidism. This can be because the lump is not thyroid tissue (for example being an abscess, lymph tissue or parathyroid tissue) or if the thyroid lump is non-functional (not producing thyroid hormones). The medical term for this is 'euthyroid goitre'. Euthyroid means that the blood levels of thyroid hormones are within the normal (reference) range. Some cats with non-functional thyroid lumps later go on to develop hyperthyroidism. Because of this, many clinicians recommend that cats with a euthyroid goitre have a thyroid hormone blood test done every 6-12 months so that those developing hyperthyroidism can be treated promptly.

- Cardiovascular abnormalities – problems relating to the heart and circulation:

  – A rapid heart rate – often faster than 220 beats per minute at a veterinary clinic when healthy cats usually have a heart rate less than 180. The medical term for a fast heart rate is tachycardia.

  – A heart murmur audible when listening to the chest with a stethoscope.

– Evidence of high blood pressure – for example damage to the eyes such as retinal detachment – can be seen in some hyperthyroid cats.

– Evidence of congestive heart failure – for example breathlessness and crackly lung sounds in cats with pulmonary oedema (fluid on the lungs) and/or a pleural effusion (fluid in the chest cavity). This is a rare complication of hyperthyroidism.

– Even if weight loss has not been noticed by an owner or care provider, it's important to check the cat's weight and body condition score (BCS). The BCS is a measure of whether the cat's weight is normal, increased or decreased for their size. Many cats are good at 'hiding' weight loss so it is sometimes only evident when they are placed on the scales.

Are there other illnesses which can mimic hyperthyroidism?

You or your veterinary surgeon may be suspicious of a diagnosis of hyperthyroidism if your cat is showing several of the clinical signs reported above. For example, weight loss in spite of a normal or increased appetite is one of the most common reasons that hyperthyroidism is suspected. However there are other illnesses which can produce similar symptoms – common examples would include:

- Polyphagia: an increased appetite can also be caused by illnesses such as diabetes mellitus ('sugar diabetes'),

SECTION 2 | explaining the science of hyperthyroidism

An increased hunger can be seen with a number of medical conditions including diabetes mellitus, inflammatory bowel disease and hyperthyroidism.

inflammatory bowel disease and some liver and pancreas problems.

- Polydipsia and polyuria: an increased thirst and amount of urine produced can be seen with other illnesses including diabetes mellitus and chronic kidney disease.

- Weight loss is a very common symptom of many illnesses and, even in an older cat, cannot be taken to indicate hyperthyroidism. Common causes of weight loss in older cats include chronic kidney disease, diabetes mellitus, cancer and bowel disorders.

- Hyperactivity and restlessness can be seen with brain disorders (for example cancers) and with behavioural problems.

- High blood pressure can be seen with a number of other problems but most common is chronic kidney disease.

How is hyperthyroidism diagnosed?

A vital starting component to making the diagnosis is taking a very thorough patient history as this is where clues of the underlying illness (such as polydipsia, polyuria and polyphagia) may become apparent. A patient history involves collecting as much information as possible about your cat and its illness.

After the history, a clinical examination is performed. During this procedure, further clues as to the cause of the illness (such as a heart murmur and rapid heart rate) may be detected.

In those cats where a diagnosis of hyperthyroidism is suspected on the basis of the history and/or clinical examination, it is likely that your veterinary surgeon will recommend further tests to confirm the diagnosis. In most cats, measurement of thyroid hormone levels is sufficient to confirm the diagnosis although other tests are highly desirable, as discussed below.

1. Blood hormone tests

It is essential that the diagnosis of hyperthyroidism is confirmed on blood testing to ensure that the correct treatment is given. A diagnosis cannot be made on clinical grounds alone – for

SECTION 2 | explaining the science of hyperthyroidism

example, occasionally cats will have a goitre but will not be suffering from hyperthyroidism.

- Total thyroxine or total T4 levels: this test is most commonly used to confirm a diagnosis of hyperthyroidism. Levels of thyroxine, also known as T4 (or tetraiodothyronine), are increased in the vast majority of hyperthyroid cats so this is usually a very simple way of confirming the diagnosis and estimating its severity. The reference range for T4 levels is included in the table on page 23. Sometimes, particularly in early cases of hyperthyroidism, a normal total T4 value will be received in a cat that has this illness. This can be because levels of the hormone fluctuate and, in early disease, this variation from day to day may mean that sometimes the result is within the reference range. If your vet suspects this possibility they may suggest repeating the total T4 test a few days or weeks later. In most cases this is the easiest way of confirming that the cat has hyperthyroidism. Presence of other illnesses (such as diabetes mellitus and chronic kidney disease) can reduce the blood levels of total T4 and in some cats this can reduce the T4 levels into the reference range (i.e. giving a falsely normal result). This phenomenon is known as 'sick euthyroid' and defines the situation where other illnesses suppress the levels of thyroid hormones. Where possible, treatment of any concurrent illness helps to increase the total T4 levels and can make diagnosis of hyperthyroidism more straightforward. T4 levels are used to monitor effectiveness of treatment for hyperthyroidism as discussed on pages 56-63.

Diagnosis of hyperthyroidism is not always straightforward – sometimes it is necessary to do several tests to diagnose this condition.

SECTION 2 | explaining the science of hyperthyroidism

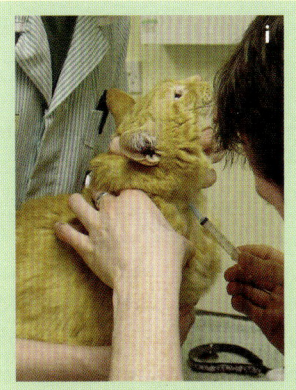
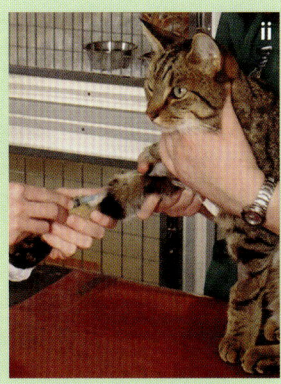

Blood is normally collected from the jugular vein (i). The cephalic vein, in the front leg (ii) is another option.

- Free thyroxine (fT4) by equilibrium dialysis: in some cats, this additional test can be helpful in confirming the diagnosis of hyperthyroidism. Free T4 testing is more sensitive (identifies more hyperthyroid cats) than the total T4 test although it can occasionally falsely diagnose hyperthyroidism. For this reason the free T4 is not generally recommended as the first test for hyperthyroidism. The reference levels of free T4 are contained in the table on page 23. Some vets routinely perform both a total and free T4 test when diagnosing hyperthyroidism in their patients. fT4 is not usually used for monitoring effectiveness of treatment for hyperthyroidism. Levels of fT4 can be affected by other illnesses and much less is known about the usefulness of this test in monitoring treated cats.

- Thyroid function tests: very occasionally, the total T4 and free T4 results will not give a clear answer and other tests may be required to try and confirm a diagnosis of hyperthyroidism. These tests include the T3 suppression and TRH stimulation tests. Of the two, the T3 suppression test is currently thought to be most reliable in diagnosing hyperthyroid cats. Results obtained with both of these tests can be affected by concurrent illnesses and this can make interpretation of results very difficult in some patients.

  – T3 suppression test: in this test, cats are medicated for a few days with a form of thyroid hormone called T3. The T3 is given as an oral pill with the cat either in a veterinary hospital or at home. Blood samples are collected before T3 treatment is started and then a few days later, after a short course of treatment has been given. In normal cats, giving extra T3 switches off the thyroid so blood levels of thyroid hormones (total T4) fall. Hyperthyroid cats are resistant to the effects of T3 so their levels of T4 remain the same (or only fall very slightly).

  – TRH stimulation test: in this test, cats are given a substance which, in normal cats, causes the release of T4 from the thyroid gland. The TRH is given as an intravenous injection (injection into a vein) and the test requires the cat to have a blood sample before the injection and four hours later. The second blood sample shows a rise in T4 levels in normal cats. Hyperthyroid cats resist the effects of TRH and so the T4 levels remain the same (or only slightly increase).

SECTION 2 | explaining the science of hyperthyroidism

2. Blood tests

Haematology (assessing the blood count, numbers and types of white blood cells and platelets) and biochemistry (assessing liver and kidney function, blood salt levels and protein levels) are recommended, where possible. Although these tests will not specifically diagnose hyperthyroidism, they are helpful in several ways:

- Looking for clues of hyperthyroidism: for example, many cats with hyperthyroidism have increased blood levels of liver enzymes (for example ALT, ALP). This is a common way that hyperthyroid cats are picked up during routine screening tests – for example in an older cat having a blood test to check that they are well enough to have an anaesthetic for dental treatment. Other abnormalities that may be seen on routine haematology and biochemistry in a hyperthyroid cat include:

  – A leucocytosis: increase in the total number of white blood cells

  – An eosinopenia: a reduction in the number of eosinophils, a specific type of white blood cell

  – Erythrocytosis: an increase in the total number of red blood cells and haemoglobin (Hb)

  – Hyperphosphataemia: an increase in blood phosphate levels (usually mild)

  – Hypokalaemia: a reduction in blood potassium levels (usually mild)

It is important to note that none of these changes are diagnostic for hyperthyroidism – all of the abnormalities listed above can occur with other illnesses.

- Looking for evidence of concurrent illnesses. Concurrent illnesses can affect which treatment is recommended for a hyperthyroid cat and also the cat's likely long-term outlook (the prognosis). Identifying concurrent illnesses early ensures the best chance of managing these and giving your cat the best quality and length of life possible.

The most common concurrent illness seen is chronic kidney disease. Unfortunately the tests currently available to test for this are not perfect and it can be quite difficult to assess kidney function in hyperthyroid cats. For example the normal measures of kidney function – the protein breakdown products urea and creatinine, and urine concentration – can all be affected by thyroid disease:

– Urea tends to be high as a hyperthyroid cat often eats excessively and consumes lots of protein. This may falsely increase the worry that a hyperthyroid cat has kidney disease.

– Creatinine tends to be low as hyperthyroid cats are thin and have very little muscle (creatinine comes from muscle turnover). This can be misleading by falsely suggesting that the cat has good kidney function.

SECTION 2 | explaining the science of hyperthyroidism

> **Diabetes mellitus is another illness that is common in older cats. Clinical signs of diabetes mellitus and hyperthyroidism are often very similar, with an increased thirst and weight loss in spite of a good appetite being most common.**

- The measure of urine concentration, urine specific gravity (USG), can be affected by thyroid disease. In healthy cats the USG is greater than 1.040. Concentrations below 1.035 are taken as one of the indications of kidney disease. In hyperthyroid cats, the ability to produce concentrated urine is compromised and USGs below this figure can be obtained from cats that have healthy kidneys. USG is discussed in more detail in the urinalysis section.

- The erythrocytosis seen in some hyperthyroid cats can 'hide' an anaemia (lack of red blood cells) that might be present in a cat with kidney disease.

Diabetes mellitus is another illness that is common in older cats. Clinical signs of diabetes mellitus and hyperthyroidism are often very similar, with an increased thirst and weight loss in spite of a good appetite being most common. Some cats suffer from both illnesses at the same time. Hyperthyroidism increases the likelihood of diabetes developing since thyroid hormones interfere with the way insulin (the hormone that regulates blood sugar levels) is able to work. This interference can lead to development of diabetes mellitus. In those cats that are already diabetic, subsequent development of hyperthyroidism can make management of their diabetes more difficult. Diagnosis of diabetes is often more difficult in hyperthyroid cats. Firstly, both conditions are often associated with similar biochemistry abnormalities (e.g. an increase in liver enzymes). Secondly, one of the diagnostic tests for diabetes mellitus (the fructosamine test) can be affected by hyperthyroidism. Fructosamine is a measure of the blood sugar levels over a period of a few weeks and blood levels of fructosamine are high in cats with untreated diabetes mellitus. Hyperthyroid cats tend to have lower levels of fructosamine due to their increased metabolic rate and this can sometimes be misleading by falsely suggesting that the cat is not diabetic. Diagnosis of hyperthyroidism can also be more difficult in diabetic cats since the thyroid hormone levels can be reduced by presence of a concurrent illness.

■ Establishing 'baseline' values. The majority of hyperthyroid cats will require at least short-term medication to treat their thyroid disease and whilst serious side-effects are rare, some of these can be detected when monitoring blood test results. It is therefore important to have pre-treatment or 'baseline' information available on each patient, where possible. Following treatment of hyperthyroidism, there may be a decline in kidney function. Unfortunately this is

SECTION 2 | explaining the science of hyperthyroidism

unpredictable and there are no tests that can be done before treatment is started that will tell you whether this is likely to occur. This issue is discussed in more detail on pages 33-34. Pre-treatment screening tests help to establish a baseline for monitoring kidney function once treatment is started.

Collection of blood samples should not be a stressful event for a cat. Blood is most easily collected from the jugular vein which is the largest vein and is located in the cat's neck. Alternatively blood can be collected from a cephalic vein which is a smaller vein, found on the front surface of the forelimbs or the medial saphenous vein which is found on the inside surface of the hind limbs.

Different laboratories have different reference ranges for blood test values and, different countries use different units which further confuses matters. The two types of unit measurements used are:

- Conventional units: used by some countries including the USA

- SI units: used by most countries including the UK

The table opposite gives a guide to the reference range levels which are likely to be normal for where you live.

N.B. the reference range will vary slightly between laboratories so the following is just a rough guide:

SECTION 2 | explaining the science of hyperthyroidism

Parameter	'Typical reference range' – Conventional units	'Typical reference range' – SI units
Urea	17 – 29 mg/dl	6 – 10 mmol/l
Creatinine	< 2 mg/dl	< 175 µmol/l
Phosphate	2.9 – 6.0 mg/dl	0.95 – 1.95 mmol/l
Potassium	4.0 – 5.0 mEq/l	4.0 – 5.0 mmol/l
Sodium	145 – 160 mEq/l	145 – 160 mmol/l
Calcium	8 – 10 mg/dl	2.0 – 2.5 mmol/l
Albumin	2.4 – 3.5 g/dl	24 – 35 g/l
Total protein	5.5 – 8.0 g/dl	55 – 80 g/l
Bicarbonate	18 – 24 mEq/l	18 – 24 mmol/l
Packed cell volume (PCV) or haematocrit	25 – 45 %	0.25 – 0.45
Haemoglobin (Hb)	0.8 – 1.5 g/dl	8 – 15 g/l
Alanine aminotransferase (ALT)	< 60 iu/l	< 60 iu/l
Alkaline phosphatase (ALP)	< 60 iu/l	< 60 iu/l
Cholesterol	85 – 155 mg/dl	2.2 – 4.0 mmol/l
Glucose	55 – 100 mg/dl	3.0 -5.5 mmol/l
Total Thyroxine (tT4)	1.5 – 3.5 µg/dl	20 – 45 nmol/l
Free T4 (fT4) by equilibrium dialysis	1.0 – 4.0 ng/dl	10 – 50 pmol/l

mg/dl – milligrams per decilitre
mmol/l – millimoles per litre
µmol/l – micromoles per litre
mEq/l – milliequivalents per litre
g/dl – grams per decilitre
g/l – grams per litre.

A table with conversion factors for converting SI units to Conventional units (and vice versa) is contained in the Reference section (Section 5).

SECTION 2 | explaining the science of hyperthyroidism

3. Urinalysis

Analysis of a urine sample is very helpful in cats with hyperthyroidism although, as with haematology and biochemistry, this test will not confirm the diagnosis. The main usefulness of urinalysis is in:

- Checking for concurrent illnesses: Urinalysis can be helpful in diagnosing diabetes mellitus – diabetic cats will have glucose (sugar) present in their urine sample. Stress may also occasionally cause some glucose to be present in a urine sample. A urinalysis is also helpful in assessing your cat's ability to produce concentrated urine. Cats with severe chronic kidney disease will often produce dilute urine which can be identified on a specific gravity (USG) test. However, hyperthyroidism also reduces the cat's ability to produce concentrated urine – although not usually as severely – so this test is not always easy to interpret.

- Checking for urinary tract infections (UTIs): recent studies have shown that a significant proportion of cats with hyperthyroidism are vulnerable to UTIs. For example, one study showed that 12% of hyperthyroid cats suffered from UTIs. Unfortunately, many cats with urinary infections do not show specific clinical signs (i.e. the infection is 'silent') and may only show vague clinical signs such as weight loss and lethargy. A small proportion of cats with urinary infections show clinical signs of cystitis including urgency to pass urine, passing small amounts of urine very frequently and passing bloody/smelly urine. It is important to identify and treat any of these additional problems, as it will help to make your cat feel as well as possible.

Urine samples can be collected in a variety of ways:

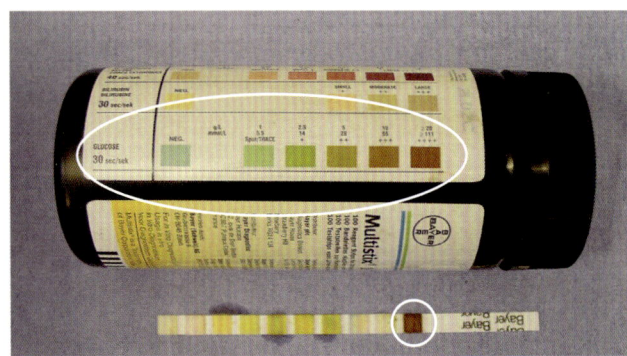

This cat has glucose present in the urine – detected since the circled pad has changed in colour from pale aqua to dark brown.

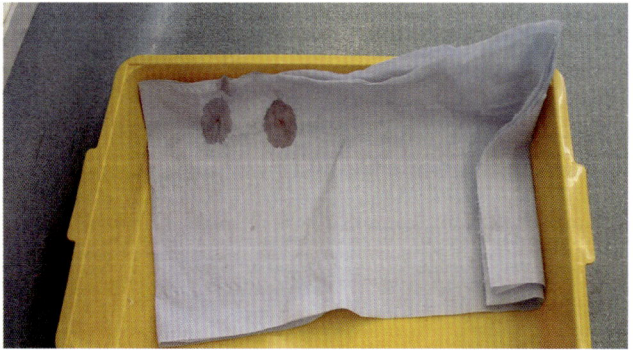

If your cat is passing small amounts of bloody urine then this may be a sign of a bacterial urinary tract infection.

SECTION 2 | explaining the science of hyperthyroidism

- **Cystocentesis**: this is the procedure by which urine is collected using a needle and syringe. The cat is gently held and the needle is passed through the skin of the tummy into the bladder. This is not a painful procedure and allows collection of a sterile (free from bacterial contamination) sample which is ideal for the tests needed.

- **Catheter samples**: urine can be collected using a catheter which is passed through the urethra (the tube from the outside of the cat to the bladder). Unfortunately this is not an appropriate technique for urine collection in most cats as it requires sedation (using drugs to provide a state of calm and muscle relaxation) or anaesthesia (using drugs to provide a state of unconsciousness, muscle relaxation and loss of pain sensation). A catheter is only appropriate as a method for urine collection if it needs to be placed for other reasons.

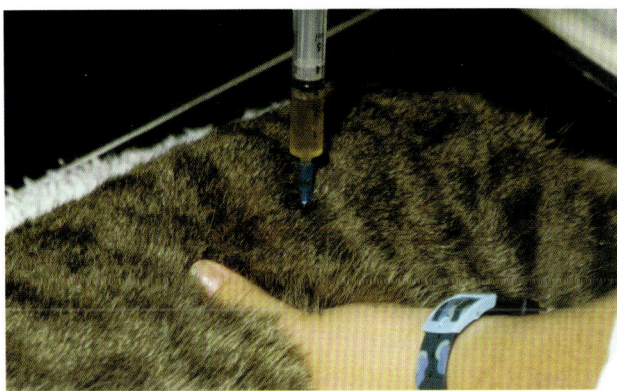

Cystocentesis is a commonly used technique to collect a urine sample. This is a procedure which is well tolerated by cats and can be done with them fully conscious, gently restrained by a nurse.

- **Free catch samples**: urine can be collected from an empty litter tray or one containing non-absorbent cat litter. Lots of different types of non-absorbent cat litter are available (for example Mikki and Katkor brands) or cheaper alternatives can be used (e.g. clean aquarium gravel, chopped up plastic bags). Once the cat has urinated, the urine can be collected using a syringe or pipette. It is important that the sample is collected as soon as possible after urination. Free catch samples are acceptable for initial assessment. For example the refractometer test which determines the concentration of the urine is not affected by the method of collection. Free catch samples are not ideal for bacterial culture or sediment examination as they will be contaminated by bacteria and debris in the litter tray and on the cat's paws. Where possible a cystocentesis sample is best for bacterial culture and sediment examination.

Non-absorbent cat litter can be used to collect urine samples at home or in the hospital.

Urine should be analysed as quickly as possible. Important urine tests in a cat with hyperthyroidism include:

- **Specific gravity measurement**: A refractometer measures the urine specific gravity (USG). Water has a specific gravity of 1.000. Normal cats usually produce urine with a specific gravity of at least 1.040. The lower the specific gravity, the more dilute the urine is. Most refractometers are designed

SECTION 2 | explaining the science of hyperthyroidism

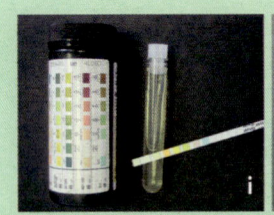 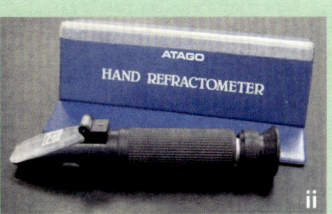

Urine is analysed in a number of ways including:

i. 'Dipstick' tests (as in people to detect sugar and protein in the urine)

ii. Urine concentration using a refractometer. Normal cats usually produce concentrated urine with a specific gravity greater than 1.040

Hyperthyroidism and chronic kidney disease are examples of two illnesses which can reduce the urine specific gravity to below 1.040.

for human urine and only measure to 1.050 so if the urine is more concentrated than this, the result will be reported as 'greater than 1.050'. Special veterinary refractometers are available in some practices and can accurately measure urine concentrations above 1.050. Cats with hyperthyroidism often have a slight reduction in their specific gravity – for example results between 1.030 and 1.040. Cats with severe kidney disease usually have a greater reduction in their specific gravity – for example results between 1.015 and 1.030.

- Urine dipstick to check for sugar (glucose), assess the acidity of the urine (urine pH) and look for other abnormalities. Dipsticks have been designed for use with human urine so are not always as reliable when used with cat urine. Glucose is present in the urine of cats with diabetes mellitus (and sometimes in the urine of cats that are stressed). Some hyperthyroid cats have concurrent diabetes mellitus.

- Sediment examination: This involves microscopic examination of a urine sample for red and white blood cells, bacteria, crystals or other material. For example this can help to diagnose a urinary tract infection. Crystals are a normal finding in cat urine, especially if the cat is fed a dry diet and also if the sample is not analysed immediately. As the temperature of urine cools (either at room temperature or in a refrigerator) crystals will form so their significance should not be over-estimated.

- Bacterial culture to see whether there is any evidence of infection. Ideally this test should be performed on urine collected by cystocentesis. When a bacterial infection is diagnosed by the laboratory they will do a sensitivity test (also referred to as a susceptibility test) to identify which antibiotics are likely to be most effective in treating the infection. This is a test which takes a few days to perform as bacterial colonies need time to grow.

4. Thyroid scintigraphy

This technique is also referred to as a technetium scan, isotope scan or radionuclide imaging. Scintigraphy is an imaging technique that can be very helpful in hyperthyroid cats. A short-acting injection of radioactive technetium is given to the cat. A few minutes later, the cat is sedated and placed on a gamma camera. The gamma camera produces a map of radioactivity in the cat's body. Technetium naturally concentrates in the thyroid gland so this allows it to be seen on the 'map' – even if it's very small. Scintigraphy is helpful in diagnosing hyperthyroidism (the thyroid will be more radioactive – 'hotter' – if it's diseased) and also locating the abnormal thyroid tissue. It is most helpful in the following situations:

SECTION 2 | explaining the science of hyperthyroidism

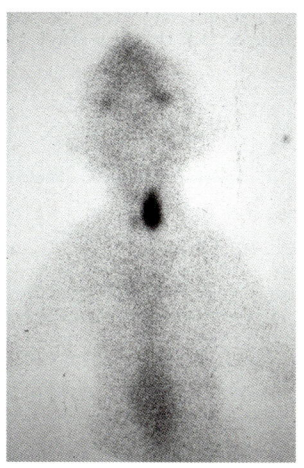 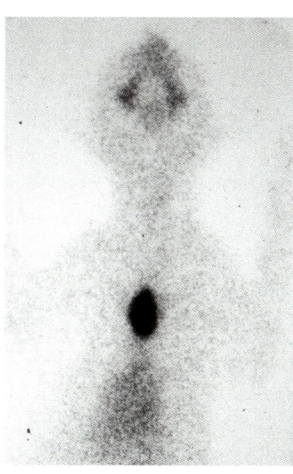

Left: Scintigraphy can be used to locate the abnormal thyroid tissue which is 'hotter' (darker) on a scan. The cat is given an injection of radioactive technetium which concentrates in the thyroid gland. A picture is taken with the cat lying on their front. In this scan, one thyroid in the neck is very 'hot' due to unilateral hyperthyroidism.

Right: This thyroid scan shows that all of the abnormal thyroid tissue is within the chest cavity. This is due to ectopic disease.

- Locating the abnormal thyroid tissue in hyperthyroid cats which do not have a goitre

- Locating the abnormal thyroid tissue in cats whose hyperthyroidism has recurred after surgical treatment

- Identifying whether the thyroid disease is affecting one or both of the thyroid lobes (uni- or bilateral disease)

- Identifying whether any ectopic thyroid tissue is affected

- Identifying whether a malignant thyroid carcinoma (cancer) has spread to other parts of the body

- The scan may be of help in deciding whether or not a malignant thyroid carcinoma will be amenable to treatment with radioiodine

Scintigraphy helps to decide which treatment is most appropriate for the cat – for example, cats with diseased ectopic thyroid tissue cannot be treated surgically. The scan procedure only takes a few minutes to perform. Unfortunately scintigraphy is only available in a few centres in the UK and around the world.

What other tests are helpful in cats with hyperthyroidism?

1. Blood pressure measurement
Blood pressure measurement is recommended in all hyperthyroid cats since high blood pressure (Systemic hypertension) is a known complication of this illness. Published reports of how commonly systemic hypertension is seen in hyperthyroid cats have varied enormously but most clinicians estimate that 15% of their hyperthyroid patients have high blood pressure. Systemic hypertension is often referred to as 'the silent killer' in people as it is common to show no outward signs of this condition before severe problems strike. High blood pressure is especially damaging to the eyes, brain and nervous system, heart and kidneys. Some cats with high blood pressure will show clinical signs including:

SECTION 2 | explaining the science of hyperthyroidism

- Eye problems such as bleeding into the eye, dilatation of the pupils (the black slit in the centre of the eye becomes very large and round), difficulty seeing and blindness. Sudden blindness is an emergency – prompt treatment can be successful in returning some vision although, sadly, many cats will remain blind for the rest of their life.

- Neurological signs such as collapse and seizures (fits) or behavioural changes (e.g. pacing aimlessly, night-time miaowing or yowling, showing signs of dementia).

- Damage to the heart resulting in development of a heart murmur and, in a very small number of cats, congestive heart failure. Signs of heart failure most commonly include lethargy and breathlessness.

- Damage to the kidneys may worsen or cause chronic kidney disease. Signs of kidney disease include a loss of appetite, weight loss, lethargy and an increased thirst and volume of urine produced.

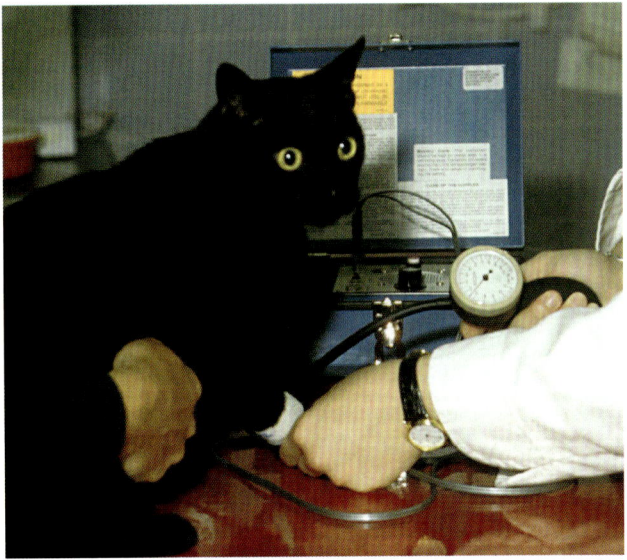

Blood pressure is most accurately measured using a Doppler machine and is a procedure which is very well tolerated by fully conscious cats. A cuff attached to a pressure gauge (called a sphygmomanometer) is placed on a forelimb or the tail; a separate sensor (the Doppler probe) is used to detect the pulse below the cuff. The cuff is inflated until the pulse signal disappears and then deflated slowly. The systolic blood pressure (higher of the two blood pressure readings we get when our own blood pressure is measured) is the pressure at which the pulse is first detectable.

Systemic hypertension is a very serious condition and it is vital that it is diagnosed and treated quickly and effectively. Systemic hypertension is diagnosed by measuring blood pressure – this is a procedure which can be done in most practices. If facilities are not available to measure blood pressure, then your vet may refer you to another practice or to a specialist so that this test can be done. Examination of the eyes can be extremely helpful when checking for signs of hypertension – your vet may be able to see abnormalities such as bleeding into the eye or retinal detachment (where the retina – the 'seeing' layer of tissue at the back of the eye – lifts off). It is currently recommended that systolic blood pressure (the higher of the two blood pressure readings) is kept below 160 – 170 mmHg (mmHg is the abbreviation for millimetres of mercury) in cats with hyperthyroidism. Readings persistently above 180 mmHg risk potentially permanent organ damage. The most helpful drugs for treating high blood pressure are amlodipine (a human drug

SECTION 2 | explaining the science of hyperthyroidism

manufactured by Pfizer as Istin in the UK, Norvasc in the US) and Angiotensin Converting Enzyme (ACE) inhibitors such as benazepril (for example Fortekor, manufactured by Novartis).

2. Diagnostic imaging

Diagnostic imaging is the term that refers to imaging techniques such as radiography (x-rays) and ultrasound. Radiographs can be helpful in identifying a number of problems:

- Heart problems can be seen as a consequence of hyperthyroidism and, in a very small number of cats, this leads to congestive heart failure. Affected cats may have abnormalities visible on radiographs including enlargement of the heart, congestion of the lungs and presence of free fluid in the chest and/or abdomen.

- Concurrent illnesses such as cancers may be visible on x-rays of the chest and/or abdomen.

- In those cats where the goitre cannot be felt, x-rays can sometimes be helpful in locating the abnormal thyroid tissue.

In most cats sedation is needed to obtain good quality radiographs of the chest and abdomen.

Ultrasound examination can be very helpful in some patients including the following situations:

- In those cats with a very large goitre, ultrasound may identify that the lump is fluid filled (the medical term for this is 'cystic').

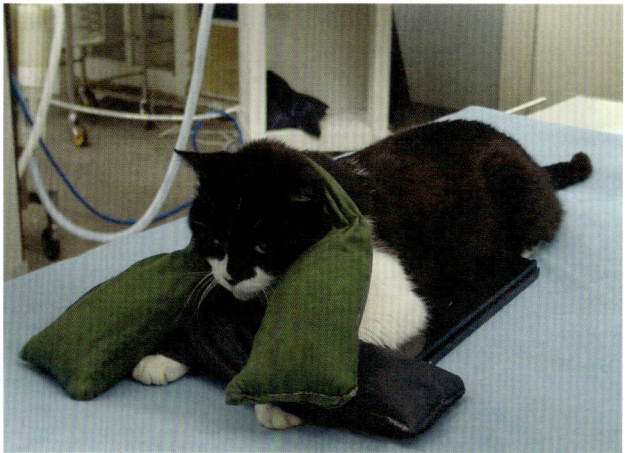

A chest x-ray can be helpful in diagnosing heart problems associated with hyperthyroidism. This cat has been sedated and is being positioned for a dorsoventral chest x-ray.

- Ultrasound of the heart is helpful in assessing the severity of any heart disease present in a hyperthyroid cat. A heart ultrasound test is called echocardiography or an echocardiogram. Most commonly, the left ventricle chamber of the heart will be thickened (referred to as left ventricular hypertrophy, LVH) and the left atrium may be enlarged (dilated). Sometimes, this condition is referred to as hyperthyroid heart disease or, less accurately, as hypertrophic cardiomyopathy (HCM). True HCM is a separate condition where there is no known cause to the heart changes. In many hyperthyroid cats, the LVH does not cause significant heart problems and there is no heart failure. The changes to the heart chambers often cause a murmur or a 'gallop rhythm' which can be heard when listening to the chest with a stethoscope. Cats with a gallop rhythm have three or

SECTION 2 | explaining the science of hyperthyroidism

four audible heart sounds instead of the normal two (lub-dub), thus sounding similar to a galloping horse. Although not always an indicator of disease, gallop rhythms are most often heard in cats with heart disease (cardiomyopathy) or high blood pressure. A gallop rhythm is one indication that the heart is not able to fill with blood as well as it should. A small percentage of hyperthyroid cats will suffer from congestive heart failure where the heart is no longer able to cope with its increased workload. Heart failure can cause congestion of the blood vessels in the lungs, pulmonary oedema (fluid within the lung tissue) and fluid production in the chest and/or abdominal cavity. Fluid in the chest cavity is called a pleural effusion; fluid in the abdomen is called ascites. The most common signs of heart failure are breathlessness due to pulmonary oedema and/or a pleural effusion.

- Ultrasound of any abnormalities found on an x-ray can help to define what these are and their significance to the cat's health.

- Ultrasound of the larynx can be helpful in diagnosing laryngeal paralysis. This is a rare side-effect seen in some cats with very large goitres and in other cats following surgery to remove a thyroid mass. Cats with laryngeal paralysis may have breathing difficulties, a change in voice (altered pitch to their meow) and a cough.

- In some situations, a screening ultrasound of the abdomen is done to look for concurrent illnesses which might be difficult to diagnose using other techniques.

Ultrasound does not require sedation or anaesthesia.

3. Electrocardiogram (ECG)
In some cats, an ECG might be helpful in assessing the severity of the heart disease associated with their hyperthyroidism. For example, the heart rate should be very regular – like a metronome – but if an abnormal heart rhythm (arrhythmia) is heard when listening with a stethoscope, an ECG can be helpful in understanding the cause of this and whether it needs treatment.

4. Thyroid biopsy and cytology
A biopsy involves collection and laboratory analysis of a sample of tissue such as the thyroid. Biopsies can be collected in three main ways:

- Fine needle aspirate (FNA): the technique by which a sample of cells is extracted from the thyroid using a needle inserted through the skin. This procedure is relatively safe ('non-invasive') but often will not give enough information as to the precise nature of the disease.

- Needle core biopsy: the technique by which a cylinder of tissue is obtained using a special needle inserted through the skin (under the guidance of ultrasound). This provides more tissue than an FNA but even so may not provide sufficient tissue to always make an accurate diagnosis. Needle core biopsies can only be done on very large goitres – they are not safe to perform on a smaller goitre. If done on a normal or small goitre, the biopsy needle risks causing damage to other

SECTION 2 | explaining the science of hyperthyroidism

important structures in the area of the thyroid such as blood vessels and nerves.

- Surgical biopsy: the technique by which the whole thyroid (excisional biopsy) or a portion of the gland (incisional biopsy) is removed via surgery. This provides the best sample of tissue for a pathologist to examine but involves general anaesthesia (deep sedation can be sufficient for the other two techniques) and the associated surgical and anaesthetic risks.

In general, biopsies are not commonly performed as:

- In most cats with thyroid disease, the biopsy results will not affect the treatment that the cat needs.

- The procedure requires sedation or anaesthesia which can be risky in some patients.

A thyroid biopsy is indicated in those cats where a malignant thyroid tumour (cancer) is suspected. This is since the treatment required for these patients is very different to that for 'routine' cases and prompt treatment improves the long-term outlook with this illness. Examples of situations where a biopsy might be indicated therefore include:

- Where malignant thyroid disease is suspected on clinical examination, for example if the thyroid lump feels very adherent (stuck) to the tissues of the neck.

> **If other illnesses are suspected then your vet may recommend that additional tests are performed.**

- Where hyperthyroidism has recurred following previous surgery – this is another situation when a malignant thyroid problem could be to blame.

- In cats with multiple thyroid lumps. In this situation it is not always easy to determine if all of the lumps are thyroid or whether other tissues (such as the parathyroid glands and lymph tissue) could be involved.

- In cats where scintigraphy has been performed and has suggested that the disease could be cancerous.

Where possible, the thyroid tissue removed from cats having surgical treatment for 'routine' hyperthyroidism (the benign disease) should be sent to a pathologist for analysis to double check that a malignant cancer is not being ignored.

5. Other tests

If other illnesses are suspected then your vet may recommend that additional tests are performed. For example, if the liver enzymes are very high then your vet may suggest that a liver ultrasound examination is performed. In those cats that have a goitre but normal thyroid hormone levels, other tests suggested may include blood calcium and phosphate levels and assessment of parathyroid gland function.

SECTION 2 | explaining the science of hyperthyroidism

What does treatment of a hyperthyroid cat involve?

The approach to treatment of hyperthyroidism involves:

1. Providing treatment for the thyroid disease
This will be discussed in more detail below.

2. Providing treatment for known complications of the thyroid disease
Some hyperthyroid cats need additional medication for complications associated with their hyperthyroidism. For example, high blood pressure (systemic hypertension) is seen in a significant proportion of hyperthyroid cats and requires specific treatment with drugs like amlodipine (a human drug manufactured by Pfizer in the UK as Istin, Norvasc in the US) and/or ACE inhibitors such as benazepril (for example Fortekor, manufactured by Novartis).

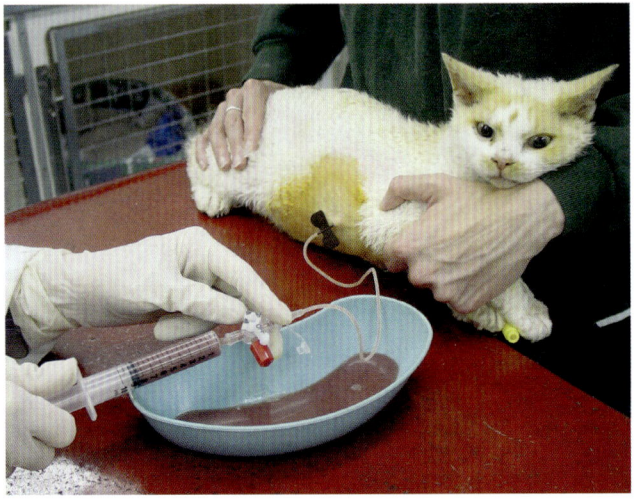

Thoracocentesis (draining the chest) may be needed in cats suffering from congestive heart failure associated with their hyperthyroidism.

If your cat has been diagnosed with a bacterial urinary tract infection then a course of antibiotics will be recommended. The type of antibiotic and length of course depends on factors including the type of infection and results of the bacterial culture and sensitivity test. The sensitivity test evaluates the ability of several different antibiotics to slow or stop the growth of the bacteria in laboratory conditions. Where concurrent kidney disease is also present, it is not unusual to prescribe a six week course of antibiotics. Successful treatment of some infections requires repeat and/or prolonged courses of treatment and your vet may recommend that repeat bacterial cultures are performed on urine samples periodically to monitor progress. Unfortunately antibiotic resistance can occur necessitating a change in the type of antibiotic prescribed.

Hyperthyroid cats with heart complications may need additional treatment such as:

- Diuretics to help treat congestive heart failure, for example, furosemide (Dimazon, Frusedale, Frusecare and Lasix are examples of trade names of this drug).

SECTION 2 | explaining the science of hyperthyroidism

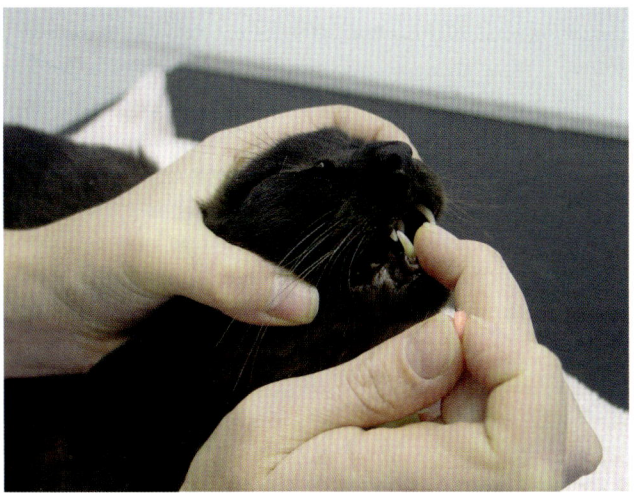

Antithyroid medication is rapidly effective in reducing blood thyroid hormone levels to the normal range.

3. Providing treatment for additional concurrent illnesses

Since hyperthyroidism is a condition which is common in older cats, it is not unusual for them to have more than one medical problems. Other common illnesses in older cats include chronic kidney disease and diabetes mellitus ('sugar diabetes'). If present, these conditions also require treatment.

How is hyperthyroidism treated?

There are three main treatment options for hyperthyroid cats:

- Medical treatment: prescribing antithyroid drugs which block production of thyroid hormones

- Surgical treatment: removal of the diseased thyroid tissue

- Radioiodine: a form of radiotherapy that is able to treat abnormal thyroid tissue

All of these treatments are also used in people with thyroid problems. For example, 80-90% of hyperthyroid people are cured by a single, tiny dose of radioactive iodine (radioiodine).

All treatments for hyperthyroidism have the potential to worsen kidney function. This is because the hyperthyroid condition increases blood flow to the kidneys. When the hyperthyroidism is treated, the blood flow to the kidneys decreases. For many hyperthyroid cats, this return to normality is not associated with kidney problems. However, in up to 20% of patients, this

- Angiotensin Converting Enzyme inhibitors (ACE inhibitors) such as benazepril (for example Fortekor, manufactured by Novartis) to help manage heart failure.

- Beta blockers such as propranolol and atenolol to help reduce the heart rate to more acceptable levels if tachycardia (a racing heart rate) is a problem.

- Drainage of the pleural effusion via a procedure called thoracocentesis. This may be done with your cat fully conscious or after sedation. Thoracocentesis involves inserting a needle into the chest cavity so that fluid can be removed.

SECTION 2 | explaining the science of hyperthyroidism

All treatments for **hyperthyroidism** have the potential to worsen kidney function.

reduction in blood flow has the potential to 'unmask' or reveal kidney disease that was not previously known about and to worsen pre-existing kidney disease. Assessing kidney function in hyperthyroid cats is difficult for many reasons, and it is not possible to predict which patients will deteriorate into chronic kidney disease following treatment of their thyroid disease. For this reason, most clinicians prefer to treat all hyperthyroid cats with medical management in the first instance. The main advantage of this treatment is that it is reversible – in other words, if the kidney function is damaged the hyperthyroid treatment can be reduced or stopped to help the cat to cope again.

If a cat is known to have kidney disease before medical treatment is started then your vet may recommend that a lower dose of medication is used initially and that the kidney values are monitored closely on blood tests. If any problems are seen, then the dose of treatment can be lowered or even stopped.

Medical treatment is the most commonly used treatment – almost all hyperthyroid cats will initially be prescribed a course of antithyroid drugs even if they go on to have either surgical treatment or radioiodine. Medical treatment can be used on its own as a lifelong treatment for hyperthyroidism. A recent UK competition identified a cat called Sasha as the longest treated cat with antithyroid medication. Sasha had been receiving Felimazole (one of the UK veterinary licensed antithyroid medications) for seven years at the time of the competition.

SECTION 2 | explaining the science of hyperthyroidism

Medical treatment of hyperthyroidism

The class of antithyroid medications most commonly used include the thioureylenes (also known as thionamides) carbimazole and methimazole (also known as thiamazole). A third thioureylene, propylthiouracil, is used much less frequently since it causes more side-effects than the other drugs.

Carbimazole is rapidly converted into methimazole by the body so both of these drugs work in the same way. Methimazole blocks the production of the thyroid hormones T4 and T3 within the thyroid gland. The blood levels of thyroid hormones fall over a period of a few days to a few weeks (depending on how high they were to start with) until they are back in the reference range. Thioureylenes are not able to cure the thyroid disease. Continued therapy with carbimazole or methimazole is needed to ensure that the blood levels stay within the reference range. Thioureylenes can be used for short periods to stabilise patients prior to curative treatments (such as radioiodine and surgery) or can be used for the rest of the cat's life to keep the thyroid disease in remission (under control).

Both carbimazole and methimazole can be given as oral tablets, usually once or twice a day. In North America, Australia and some other locations, transdermal preparations of thioureylenes are available from some pharmacists. Transdermal preparations come as a skin cream which is usually applied to the inside of the cat's ear (a hairless area). The medication is absorbed through the skin and into the blood stream. Transdermal antithyroid medications can take longer to be effective than the oral form.

Transdermal medications are controversial – there is much less evidence to demonstrate their effectiveness. The skin normally forms a barrier to stop substances from entering the body so this might not always be a good way of delivering a drug to the blood stream. There are no licensed (veterinary authorised) transdermal antithyroid medications available in the UK.

Advantages of thioureylenes include:

- The drugs are readily available through all vet practices so it's easy to get hold of them and start the treatment.

- This treatment is initially less expensive than the curative treatment options (surgery and radioiodine) although lifelong treatment can be as expensive (or more expensive, if your cat lives a long time on this treatment).

- The treatment starts to work very quickly and most cats have normal blood levels of thyroid hormones within three weeks of starting the therapy.

- Most cats suffer no side-effects of treatment, even with very long-term use. Many cats will remain stable for years when treated with these drugs.

- The treatment can be titrated 'to effect' – in other words, the dose of treatment can be varied to suit the individual cat. This is especially helpful in some cats that have concurrent illnesses, most important of which is chronic kidney disease.

SECTION 2 | explaining the science of hyperthyroidism

- The treatment is reversible which is an advantage in cats with concurrent kidney disease where any treatment for hyperthyroidism can cause a worsening in their kidney function.

- Medical management is a good way of stabilising a patient in preparation for surgical treatment or whilst awaiting radioiodine. Stabilised patients are in a better state to cope with anaesthesia and surgery.

- Unlike the other two treatments (surgery and radioiodine), no hospitalisation, sedation or anaesthesia is required.

- Since this is a non-surgical treatment, there are none of the possible side-effects associated with an operation (as discussed later).

- Hypothyroidism (an underactive thyroid) is rare with medical treatment and can be easily corrected by reducing the dose of medication. Hypothyroidism is discussed later in this book.

As with all drugs, the thioureylenes can cause side-effects in some cats although these are not common. Side-effects usually occur within the first three months of treatment and include:

- Mild side-effects: seen in approximately 10 – 20% of cats treated with either carbimazole or methimazole and include

  – Loss of appetite

  – Nausea and vomiting

  – Lethargy

  – Mild side-effects on haematology such as eosinophilia (an increase in the number of a type of white blood cell called an eosinophil)

In most cats with these side-effects, the clinical signs are mild and only last a few days. In some cats, the side effects are more severe and may necessitate stopping treatment and having a few days off therapy. Many of these cats can tolerate the treatment if it is re-started, perhaps at a lower starting dose and then gradually increased.

- Severe side effects: seen in less than 5% of treated cats include

  – Persistent and more severe tummy upsets (nausea, vomiting and loss of appetite are most common)

  – Dermatitis – inflammation of the skin, often affecting the head and neck area. This can be intensely itchy and affected cats may cause a lot of trauma to themselves when scratching

  – Blood clotting problems

  – More serious abnormalities on haematology, for example:

SECTION 2 | explaining the science of hyperthyroidism

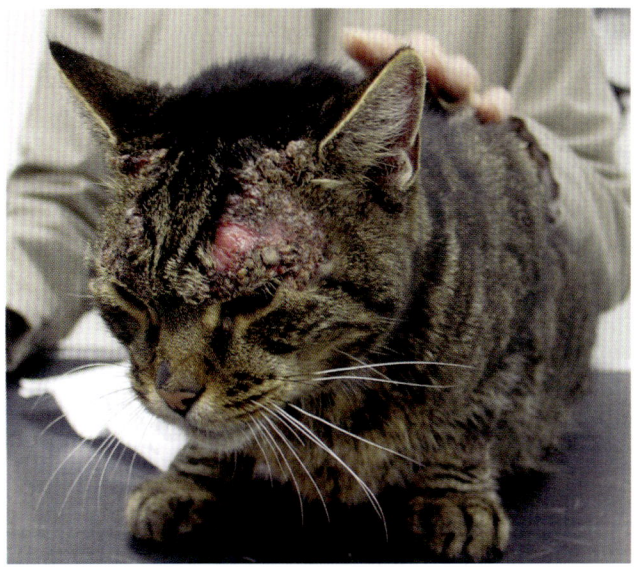

A rare side-effect of thioureylene drugs is development of intensely itchy skin, especially in the head and neck area. The severe itch can result in a lot of self-trauma to this area. This side-effect completely cures once the thioureylene treatment is stopped although it can take a few weeks for the skin to fully recover.

- Thrombocytopenia: low platelet numbers which can cause spontaneous bruising and bleeding

- Leucopenia: low white blood cell numbers which can leave the cat very vulnerable to infections

- Immune-mediated haemolytic anaemia: a reaction to the antithyroid medication which causes the cat's immune system to attack and destroy their own red blood cells

– Liver disease (hepatopathy)

– Myasthenia gravis: a condition in which the communication between the nerves and the muscles is damaged. Affected cats are often very weak and listless, unable to hold their head up or to walk for more than a few steps at a time

In cats suffering from severe side-effects, the antithyroid medication usually needs to be stopped and an alternative treatment found. Affected cats may also require additional treatment, for example cats developing myasthenia gravis may need treatment with drugs called cholinesterase inhibitors and glucocorticoids (a form of steroid).

Disadvantages of the thioureylene agents and medical management of hyperthyroidism include:

■ The possibility of side-effects as discussed above. Some cats are unable to tolerate this type of treatment.

■ In view of the potential for side-effects, regular monitoring is recommended so that any side-effects can be identified and treated quickly. More information on long-term monitoring of patients is discussed on pages 56-60.

■ The medication does not cure the condition so treatment is required for the rest of the cat's life. Missing an occasional dose of treatment is probably not a concern but if the treatment is stopped completely, levels of thyroid hormones typically increase to hyperthyroid levels in three days or less. Continuous therapy is therefore very important.

SECTION 2 | explaining the science of hyperthyroidism

Most hyperthyroid cats treated with antithyroid medication suffer no side-effects of treatment, even with very long-term use.

- Treatment monitoring is required to ensure that the correct dose of medication is being given – some thyroids become more active over time and the dose of treatment may need to be increased.

- In cats needing life-long treatment, it can be difficult remembering to give the treatment every day and therefore some studies have suggested that medical treatment is less effective in the long term than curative treatment options such as radioiodine.

- Hyperthyroid cats can be difficult to give pills to, so long-term medication can be hard work!

- Very occasionally, some cats are resistant to the thioureylene drugs meaning that they may need very high doses or an alternative treatment to control their illness.

The main veterinary licensed (authorised) thioureylenes are:

- Methimazole: In the UK this is manufactured as the veterinary licensed product Felimazole by Dechra; manufactured as Tapazole, a human licensed product, by Lilly in the US and some other countries. Methimazole is a bitter tasting drug so is normally presented in a sugar coated tablet. Most cats need twice daily treatment to initially stabilise their illness. Once stable (euthyroid), a proportion of cats can be maintained on once a day treatment although others will need to remain on twice daily treatment. Felimazole can be given with or without food although you should try and be consistent in

SECTION 2 | explaining the science of hyperthyroidism

how you medicate your cat. For those cats that are difficult to medicate orally, hiding the pill in a small amount of food can be helpful. Since methimazole is a bitter tasting drug, the pill should not be crushed in the food. Occasionally this is necessary to achieve medication – where it is done, the advice below should be followed.

- Carbimazole is manufactured in the UK as the veterinary licensed product Vidalta by Intervet/Schering-Plough; and as a human licensed product NeoMercazole by Amdipharm in the UK and some other countries. Carbimazole is a tasteless drug so does not normally come in a sugar coated form. Vidalta is a 'sustained release' preparation which means that the carbimazole is slowly released from the tablet. Because of this, Vidalta is only needed once a day. Standard carbimazole preparations (including the human preparation NeoMercazole) have to be given two to three times a day to be effective. Since Vidalta is a sustained release product the pill needs to be taken whole – if crushed the drug will all be released immediately and not last for 24 hours. If crushing the pill is necessary, Vidalta should be given twice daily using the same overall daily dose. For example if 1 tablet once a day was originally prescribed, half a crushed tablet should be given twice daily. The absorption of Vidalta is affected by whether or not the cat has eaten so it is suggested that a stable routine is kept as to whether the tablet is given with or without food. Tablets should be given at the same time each day.

Advice on crushing methimazole and carbimazole in food:
Although not ideal, occasionally crushing methimazole or carbimazole is sometimes necessary to achieve medication. When you have to do this, you should wear gloves when crushing the pills since some people can be sensitive to antithyroid drugs. The crushed pill should be given in the smallest amount of food possible to try and ensure that the whole dose is eaten rather than being left in the food. Pregnant women should wear gloves when handling antithyroid drugs. Crushing medication constitutes 'off license' use of a veterinary authorised product and is not recommended unless this is the only way of successfully medicating your cat.

Information and tips on giving pills can be found on pages 41-43.

In the UK, strict laws exist to control the prescription of drugs to pets. These laws are aimed at protecting animals from medications which may be either unsafe or ineffective (or both). Under the Cascade system, veterinary surgeons are obliged to prescribe veterinary licensed or 'authorised' preparations (drugs which have been designed for use in animals and which have been studied in animals) where these exist. If there is no medicine authorised for treatment of a specific condition in a particular species of animal then it is legal to use alternative treatments. When this is done, a strict sequence must be followed:

SECTION 2 | explaining the science of hyperthyroidism

1. The first choice is a veterinary medicine authorised in the UK for use in another animal species

2. If this is not available then a medicine authorised in the UK for human use can be prescribed OR a veterinary medicine from another country can be imported under special import certificate

3. If neither of the above are possible then a vet, pharmacist or other 'appropriate' person can prepare a medicine for use in a patient

More detailed information can be read on: http://www.noahcompendium.co.uk/Compendium/Overview/-45043.html.

Treatment monitoring on thioureylene therapy
It is normal for treated cats to be reassessed around three weeks after starting therapy. At this time, the thyroid hormone levels are checked to see if your cat is on an adequate dose of treatment and additional tests are done to check for evidence of any side-effects such as kidney problems. Further monitoring tests are discussed on pages 56-60.

Other medical agents
Very occasionally, other medical agents may be recommended for your cat. In general these are not as effective as the thioureylenes but may be recommended for cats that have suffered severe side-effects. In most cases, the drugs listed below are only effective as a short-term treatment before surgery or radioiodine therapy can be performed:

- Stable iodine: this therapy can provide some short-term assistance in treating hyperthyroid cats by temporarily blocking production and release of thyroid hormones by the thyroid gland. Iodine tends to only be effective for up to a couple of weeks so is most helpful in stabilising a patient prior to surgery.

- Calcium ipodate and iopanoic acid: these substances work by inhibiting conversion of T4 to T3. T3 is the more potent of the two thyroid hormones. Ipodate may also have some other effects, including blocking T3 receptors which stops T3 from having an effect on tissues.

- Potassium iodate: this substance works by blocking the thyroid gland's ability to take up iodine and therefore helps to reduce blood levels of thyroid hormones. Some cats treated with this drug will suffer with an upset tummy; reducing the dose of drug can help to control this. Potassium iodate has been used successfully in combination with propranolol in stabilising hyperthyroid cats prior to surgery.

- Beta blockers: drugs such as atenolol and propranolol can help stabilise hyperthyroid cats by slowing their heart rate and improving heart function. Beta blockers can also help treat some of the signs of anxiety and nervousness shown in some hyperthyroid cats. Propranolol has been used successfully in combination with potassium iodate in stabilising hyperthyroid cats prior to surgery.

None of the treatments listed above are veterinary licensed for treatment of hyperthyroid cats.

SECTION 2 | explaining the science of hyperthyroidism

What is the best way to medicate my cat?

An illustrated guide on giving pills to a cat is on page 42. The Useful website section also contains a link to a video showing how to give pills and capsules to cats. Tablets should be given at the same time each day. If twice daily treatment is required it should be given as close to 12 hours apart as is practically possible. Three times a day medication should ideally be given eight hours apart. After any tablet or capsule medication is given the cat should be offered food or given a small amount of water (for example 1-5 ml of water by syringe) to encourage the tablet to travel to the stomach. This is to prevent tablets or capsules from sitting in the food pipe (oesophagus) for prolonged periods where they can cause irritation and potentially serious and long-lasting problems such as strictures (scarring and narrowing of the food pipe).

For those cats that are difficult to medicate orally, hiding the pill in a small amount of food can be helpful. Some cats enjoy treats such as soft cheese, butter or tuna and the pill can be hidden in here. Alternatively, you can try pill-hiding treats which are available from vets and some pet shops – these include brands like Pill Pockets (manufactured by Greenies) and Tab Pockets (manufactured by Royal Canin).

Cats receiving multiple therapies can be difficult to medicate. Medicating with multiple drugs can be made easier by using empty gelatine capsules available from a vet or pharmacist. The capsule is opened, the appropriate drugs are added and then the capsule is closed again. This means that it is possible to dose a cat with two or more medicines in one go – likely to

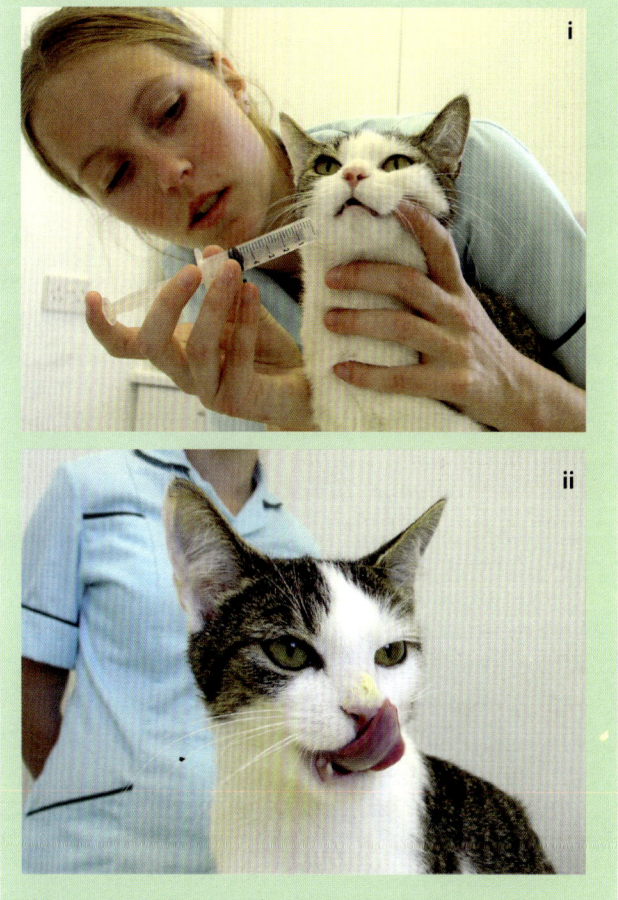

(i) Syringing a small amount of water after giving a pill or capsule helps the medication to travel to the stomach quickly and without causing any irritation to the oesophagus (food pipe). Alternatively (ii) a small amount of butter can be put on the cat's nose – licking this off also helps any pills and capsules to travel quickly to the stomach.

SECTION 2 | explaining the science of hyperthyroidism

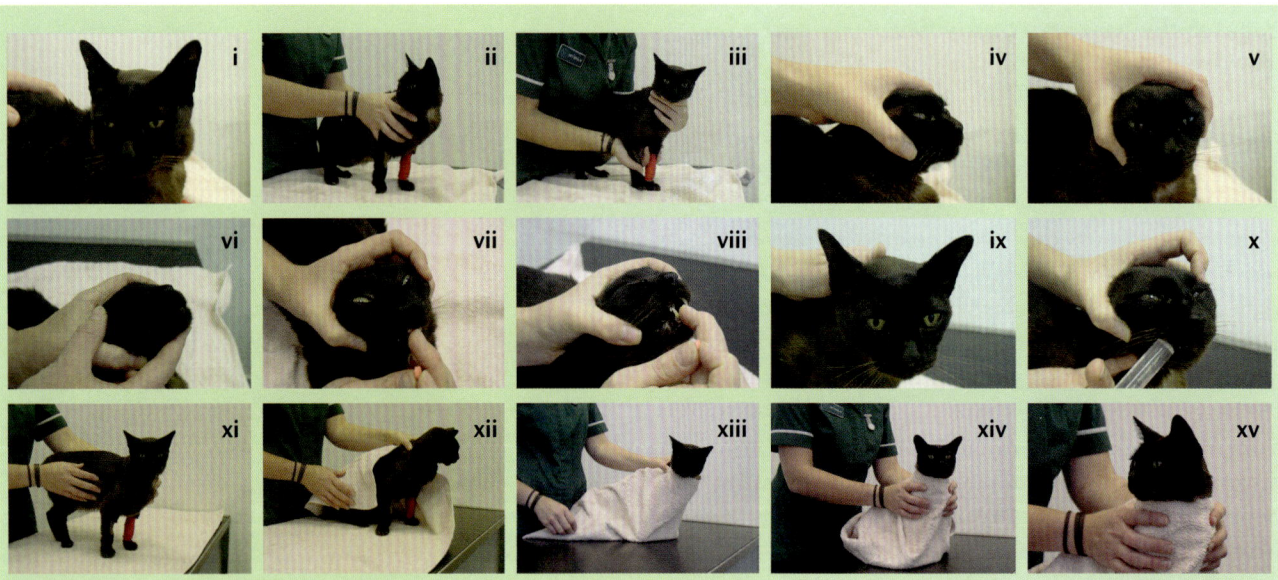

Medicating cats with pills or tablets
(i) try and ensure that your cat remains calm and relaxed; (ii) and (iii) the person restraining the cat gently holds the front legs so that they cannot come up and prevent pills being given or scratch you; (iv) and (v) make your forefingers and thumb into an arch shape and place this over the head holding the bony angles of the jaw firmly (this should not hurt your cat at all); (vi) tip your cat's head back gently so that the nose points to the ceiling; (vii) holding the pill between your thumb and forefinger gently open the jaw using your third finger; (viii) place the pill as far to the back of the mouth as possible; (ix) release your cat's head and allow them to swallow naturally, (x) syringe a small amount of water after giving the pill or allow your cat to have something to eat. (xi)–(xv) If your cat is very wriggly then placing them between your legs whilst you kneel on the floor or wrapping in a towel can help.

SECTION 2 | explaining the science of hyperthyroidism

be much more popular with the cat than giving multiple pills. Giving multiple medications can increase the risk of side-effects through drug interactions which is something for you and your vet to discuss and be aware of when working out a treatment regime for your cat. If you are finding it difficult to medicate your cat ask your vet to prioritise which treatments are most important so that you can ensure that your cat is getting the most important ones everyday.

Surgical treatment of hyperthyroidism

Surgical treatment of hyperthyroidism involves removing the abnormal thyroid tissue. This procedure is called a thyroidectomy. Thyroid surgery can be unilateral (removing the abnormal thyroid gland on one side only) or bilateral (removing both abnormal thyroid lobes). A number of different procedures have been described in cats with some surgeons preferring certain methods over others. Commonly performed techniques include the modified intra- and extra-capsular thyroidectomies.

Surgery requires anaesthesia of the patient, so where at all possible, your cat will be stabilised medically before surgery is done. This is to reduce the risks of anaesthesia that are present in a cat with hyperthyroidism.

The ideal surgery:

- Removes all of the abnormal thyroid tissue leaving no 'remnants' that could possibly re-grow.

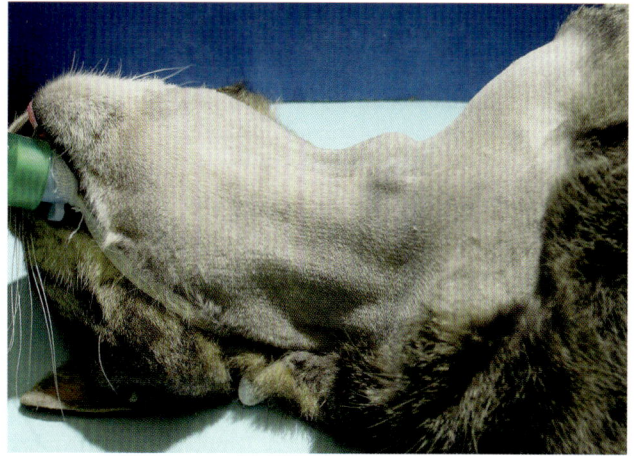

Once the cat has been anaesthetised and the neck clipped and prepared for surgery, it may be possible to see the thyroid mass/masses in the neck.

- Does not remove or damage adjacent tissues. Of particular importance are:

  – The parathyroid glands: these small glands are located very close to the thyroid tissue and help to control blood levels of calcium. Two pairs of parathyroid gland are present in each cat – one pair lying outside the thyroid gland and the other pair lying inside the capsule that surrounds the thyroid. If these delicate structures are damaged or removed during thyroid surgery, affected cats can suffer from hypocalcaemia (low blood calcium levels) which can be fatal if not treated. This condition is called hypoparathyroidism. Since this is one of the most common side-effects of surgery it is discussed separately later.

SECTION 2 | explaining the science of hyperthyroidism

– The sympathetic nervous system: nerves involved in this part of the nervous system pass close to the thyroid glands and can be damaged during surgery. Affected cats can develop temporary or permanent Horner's syndrome. This is recognised as a droopy upper eyelid, smaller pupil, a sunken eye (ptosis) and protrusion of the third eyelid (sometimes referred to as the Haws or nictitating membrane). This is a very rare potential complication of thyroid surgery and is usually temporary although it may take weeks or months to resolve.

– The recurrent laryngeal nerve: this is one of the nerves that supplies the larynx (voice box). Temporary or permanent damage can occur during surgery and is called laryngeal paralysis (paralysis of the larynx). Affected cats may have voice changes, develop noisy breathing or a cough and can have difficulty breathing. In severe cases, surgery may be required to treat the laryngeal paralysis. This is a very rare potential complication of thyroid surgery.

– Arteries and veins to and from the head and neck area: damage to these blood vessels can cause bruising of the tissue which may be visible. It is extremely rare to get any more serious side-effects associated with blood loss.

Advantages of surgical treatment include:

■ This is a curative procedure in those patients where it is possible to remove all of the abnormal thyroid tissue. After surgery, treated cats should no longer need antithyroid medication.

Horner's syndrome is a rare, and often temporary, complication that can be seen with thyroidectomy. Affected cats have a droopy upper eyelid, smaller pupil, sunken eye and protrusion of the third eyelid on the affected side. This cat has left-sided Horner's.

■ Surgery can be done quickly and most vets are very confident and competent in doing this operation.

Disadvantages of surgical treatment include:

■ Your cat may need to be hospitalised for a few days for monitoring after surgery.

■ Anaesthesia is required and this can be a problem in some

SECTION 2 | explaining the science of hyperthyroidism

cats – for example those with heart or kidney disease. An untreated hyperthyroid cat is more sensitive to certain medications used in anaesthesia so achieving control of the hyperthyroidism before surgery is very important.

- The procedure is only possible if the abnormal thyroid tissue is within the neck and therefore easily accessible by the surgeon. For those cats with ectopic thyroid tissue, other treatment methods may need to be found as the thyroid tissue may not be accessible to surgery.

- A skilled surgeon is required: not all veterinary surgeons may feel able to offer this treatment.

- Occasionally recurrence can be seen. This can be for one of several reasons listed in order of decreasing frequency:

  – A cat that has had unilateral thyroid disease (only one thyroid lobe affected) may go on to develop disease of the other thyroid lobe in the future. Cats suffering from unilateral hyperthyroidism will develop atrophy (shrinking) of the other thyroid lobe. This makes it difficult to impossible to remove normal thyroid tissue surgically as the risks of causing hypoparathyroidism are greatly increased. Bilateral thyroid disease occurs in around 70% of all hyperthyroid cats making this the most common reason for recurrence of disease.

  – A small amount of abnormal thyroid tissue is left behind during surgery. This tissue can re-grow and lead to recurrence of hyperthyroidism.

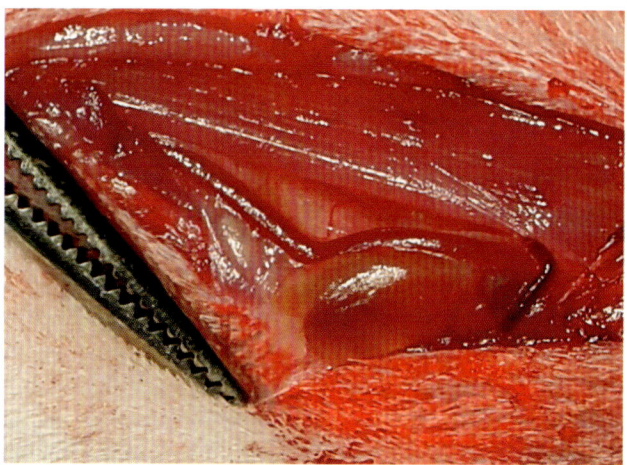

A typical thyroid mass is being removed from this cat.

  – Multiple abnormal areas of thyroid tissue (for example ectopic tissue as well as both thyroid lobes) are causing the hyperthyroidism. Abnormal thyroid tissue can be very small and difficult to feel or locate at surgery, therefore in these patients it can be difficult to guarantee that all abnormal tissue has been removed. In an ideal world, these patients are best identified prior to surgery using thyroid scintigraphy. Unfortunately scintigraphy facilities are not routinely available in most veterinary practices.

- Surgery can be associated with side-effects including those discussed on pages 43-44. Of particular importance is damage to or removal of the parathyroid tissue which causes post-operative hypoparathyroidism. This is discussed in more detail below.

SECTION 2 | explaining the science of hyperthyroidism

- Hypothyroidism (an underactive thyroid) is a rare complication that can occur with surgery. In most cats, with time, ectopic thyroid tissue can develop and take over.

What is post-operative hypoparathyroidism?

Post-operative hypoparathyroidism is the name for the situation which occurs when damage to the parathyroid glands (see above) occurs during thyroid surgery. The frequency of this side-effect varies according to the skill of the surgeon and other factors such as the size of the thyroid and how easy it is to remove. Overall, probably less than 10% of cats having thyroid surgery will suffer from this side-effect.

The parathyroid glands are very sensitive to handling and so can be easily damaged although in many cases, this is temporary. If the parathyroid glands are inadvertently removed then this too will cause hypoparathyroidism. Even in these cases, the hypoparathyroidism is usually temporary since, with time, ectopic parathyroid tissue can develop.

Hypoparathyroidism causes hypocalcaemia – low blood calcium levels – and this can be fatal.

The risk of hypoparathyroidism occurring is highest when a cat requires a bilateral thyroidectomy (removal of both thyroid lobes). For this reason, many vets prefer to 'stage' their thyroidectomies – removing one abnormal thyroid on one day and waiting for a few weeks or months before operating on the second lobe. This reduces the risk of hypoparathyroidism

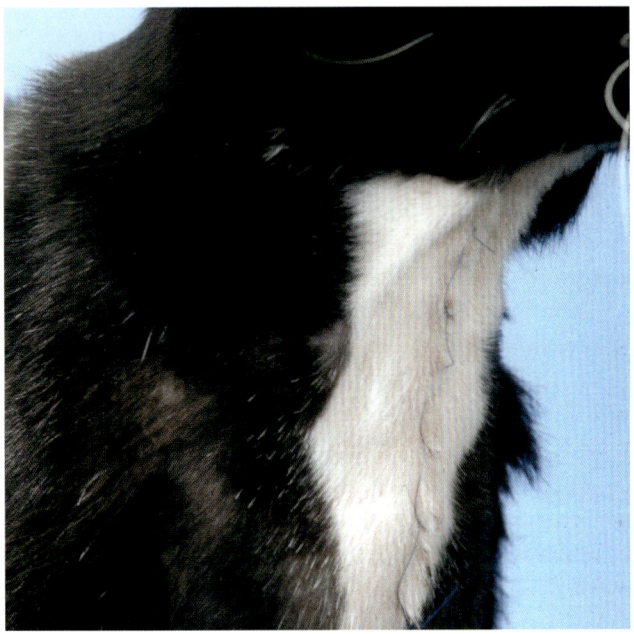

This cat has had a thyroidectomy to remove a large thyroid mass. The skin stitches are visible and need to stay in for 7-10 days to allow the wound to heal.

as only one parathyroid gland is normally required to maintain healthy blood levels of calcium.

Very occasionally hypoparathyroidism can be seen after a unilateral thyroidectomy. In these cases it is thought that handling of both sets of parathyroid glands during tissue manipulation has caused some bruising of the parathyroid glands. Bruising can cause temporary problems with calcium regulation and hence hypoparathyroidism.

SECTION 2 | explaining the science of hyperthyroidism

If your cat has a thyroidectomy, it is normal for them to be hospitalised for at least 24 hours following surgery so that their progress can be closely monitored. Monitoring usually includes blood tests for calcium levels. Signs of hypocalcaemia often develop within two to three days of surgery and include:

- Loss of appetite

- Weakness

- Anxiety

- Increased sensitivity and over-reaction to touch and sound (hyperaesthesia)

- Twitching and tremors

- Seizures (fits)

- Severely affected cats may lapse into a coma and die if not treated

Not all cats developing hypoparathyroidism need treatment – as long as the blood calcium levels do not drop too low or too quickly. In those cats that do need treatment, both calcium and vitamin D are usually required. In an emergency situation, calcium may be needed by injection. Vitamin D treatment is important as this helps calcium given by mouth to be absorbed. In many cats, after a few days of treatment, Vitamin D therapy alone is sufficient to stabilise blood calcium levels. For most affected cats, this condition is temporary with the parathyroid glands recovering over a period of days or weeks. During this period, the blood calcium levels are monitored and the dose of calcium and/or Vitamin D altered such that blood calcium levels stay at the bottom of the reference range. In most cats, the dose of treatment is gradually reduced until they no longer require calcium or Vitamin D. Most cats will need some treatment for a few months, only a very small proportion of cats will need to stay on these medications longer than this.

Radioiodine treatment of hyperthyroidism

Radioiodine (also referred to as ^{131}I) is a form of radiotherapy that is able to treat abnormal thyroid tissue. It is regarded as the 'gold standard' treatment for hyperthyroidism as it is so safe and effective.

Radioiodine contains a very small dose of radioactive iodine. The treatment is given either by oral capsule or by injection and naturally targets the thyroid tissue. Iodine is used by the thyroid gland to produce thyroid hormones. The radioactivity is able to destroy the abnormal thyroid tissue, shrinking the goitre and reducing the amount of thyroid hormones produced.

Radioiodine is regarded as the safest treatment for hyperthyroidism. The dose of radioactivity required is very low and therefore is not damaging to other tissues of the body. There is no risk of damage to the parathyroid glands or any other tissues that can be damaged by surgery. For human health and safety reasons (exposure to radioactivity), some vets prefer to sedate patients if they are injecting the radioiodine.

SECTION 2 | explaining the science of hyperthyroidism

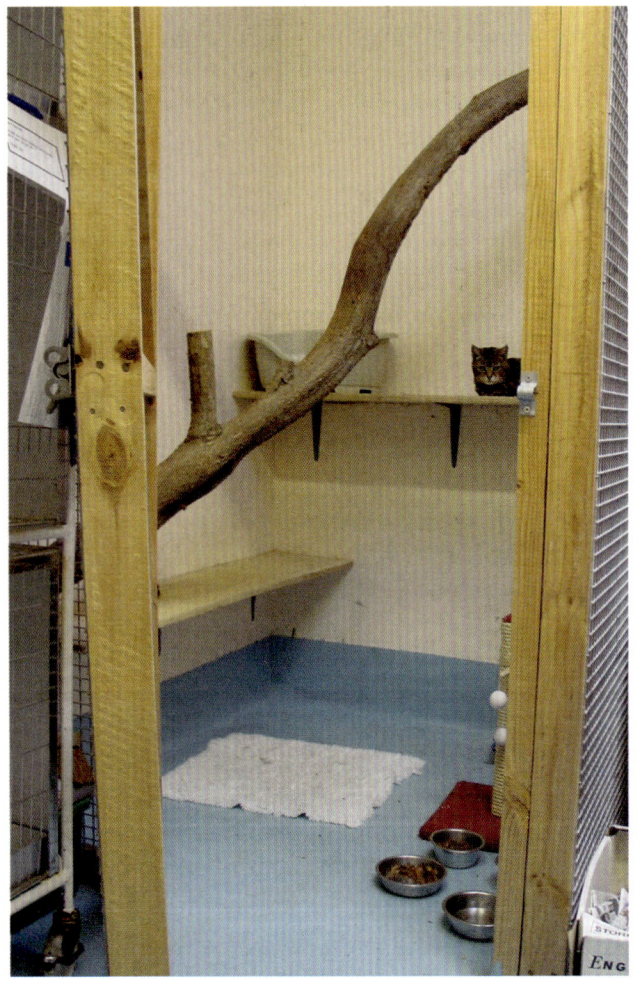

One of the University of Bristol's radioiodine units. Trees, shelves and toys are used to make the environment as stimulating as possible for the cat's hospital stay.

Hyperthyroid cats receiving antithyroid treatments such as methimazole usually need to stop this treatment one to four weeks before the radioiodine is given – the precise guidelines will vary according to which medication is being used. Treatments for high blood pressure and heart disease do not affect the effectiveness of iodine treatment so can be given continuously.

Advantages of radioiodine treatment include:

- No anaesthetic is required

- The treatment is very effective – most reports indicate that about 95% of hyperthyroid cats are cured with a single dose of radioiodine

- All abnormal hyperthyroid tissue is treated – wherever it is located in the cat. This makes radioiodine an excellent treatment for cats with ectopic thyroid disease

- Radioiodine is safe to the parathyroid glands and other tissues of the body, only the thyroid gland is being targeted by this treatment

- It is very rare for the hyperthyroidism to recur following successful treatment

- Side-effects are very rare: hypothyroidism (an underactive thyroid) is common following treatment but usually resolves with time. It is very rare for a cat to remain hypothyroid such that they need treatment for this. In those cats that do need treatment, oral thyroid hormone medication is available and

SECTION 2 | explaining the science of hyperthyroidism

can be used. Hypothyroidism is discussed in more detail later

- Radioiodine is the only treatment that is effective for many cats with thyroid carcinomas. A higher dose of radioiodine is needed in these patients (typically five to ten times the usual dose)

Disadvantages of radioiodine include:

- Since the treatment involves radioactive material, strict human health and safety controls exist in many countries where this treatment is allowed. These regulations, which vary from country to country (and from region to region) require treated cats to be hospitalised in special facilities for a period after their treatment. This is done to limit human exposure to radioactive substances. For example, in the UK, most treated cats must be kept in special hospital facilities for three to five weeks. In some US clinics, this period can be as short as three days although it is more often one to three weeks. In Australia, treated cats typically need to stay in the hospital for five to ten days.

- Because of the strict health and safety requirements, available facilities for treatment of hyperthyroid cats with radioiodine are very limited. Waiting lists at individual centres vary according to demand but you should be prepared to find that there may be a delay before treatment can be done. The Appendix contains further information on locating a radioiodine clinic in the UK, North America, Australia and New Zealand. In other regions, the best advice on locating one of these clinics is to ask your own vet or contact the closest University Veterinary School since many of these have radioiodine treatment facilities.

- Cats having this treatment need to be in relatively good health since it is not possible to handle them for at least a few days after their treatment. For example, example, cats requiring daily subcutaneous fluids for chronic kidney disease are not suitable patients for radioiodine therapy.

- In some cats, it can take several months before the full effects of the treatment can be seen. Very occasionally (less than 5-10% cases), a second treatment may be needed.

- Although side-effects are very rare with this treatment, occasionally permanent hypothyroidism (an underactive thyroid gland) can be seen. This is easily treatable with thyroid hormone supplements as described later.

Other treatments for hyperthyroidism

Other techniques that have been described for hyperthyroid cats include:

- Chemical ablation: this technique involves anaesthesia of the patient before injecting 100% ethanol (an alcohol) into the thyroid tissue, using ultrasound to guide placement of the needle. Published studies have shown that this treatment can be effective, especially in cats with unilateral disease, although multiple treatments may be necessary in some cats. Unfortunately some cats have suffered side effects to

SECTION 2 | explaining the science of hyperthyroidism

adjacent tissues such as the recurrent laryngeal nerve and sympathetic nervous system. So far, this treatment has not been as successful as existing treatments and the reported side effects can be very serious.

- Percutaneous radiofrequency heat ablation: this technique has been studied in a small number of cats. Unfortunately the treatment is only temporarily effective – on average lasting for about four months, the maximum duration reported is 18 months. Side effects can be seen associated with damage to adjacent nerve tissues such as the sympathetic nervous system and recurrent laryngeal nerve. Fortunately in many cases, these side-effects have been temporary. These side effects are explained in more detail on page 44. Repeated treatment was needed in several cats to achieve euthyroidism (reduce the thyroid hormone levels into the normal range).

At present both of these techniques are regarded as experimental procedures, still under evaluation by certain specialist clinicians.

What is hypothyroidism?

Hypothyroidism is the medical term for an underactive thyroid gland which is not producing adequate amounts of thyroid hormones. This can be seen as a congenital condition (present from birth) but is most often seen as a result of treatment for hyperthyroidism.

Blood test monitoring of medically treated hyperthyroid cats allows accurate dosing so that if a cat is being over-treated, the dose can be reduced to correct this. In cats that have had permanent treatments for their hyperthyroidism, such as iodine or surgery, transient hypothyroidism (lasting up to six months) is common and probably affects up to 30% of patients. Treatment is rarely required as the hypothyroidism completely resolves in the majority of these cats. Ectopic thyroid tissue is believed to develop and provide sufficient thyroid hormone.

Radioiodine therapy for hyperthyroidism carries the highest risk of inducing permanent hypothyroidism but this is probably only seen in less than 5% of cats.

There is one reported case of adult-onset hypothyroidism which was not caused by treatment of hyperthyroidism. In this cat, the illness was caused by an inflammatory disease affecting the thyroid gland (a disease called lymphocytic thyroiditis).

Typical signs of hypothyroidism in an adult cat include:

- Lethargy and depression

- Weight gain

- Coat changes – for example poor hair re-growth (for example if an area of the coat is clipped), hair loss over the ears, dandruff/scurf in the coat

- Constipation

- Heat seeking behaviour – hypothyroid cats may feel cold

SECTION 2 | explaining the science of hyperthyroidism

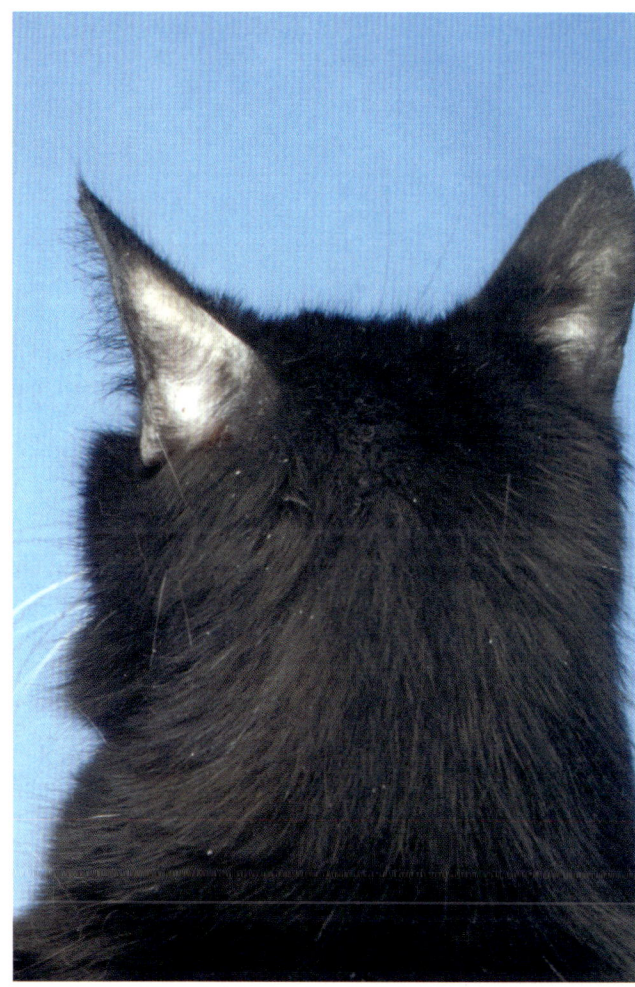

Hypothyroidism (an underactive thyroid) can be seen following treatment of hyperthyroidism. In this patient the hypothyroidism was associated with hair loss over the ears and more dandruff in the coat.

- Myxoedema – the face can appear swollen and puffy, especially around the eyes, cheeks and forehead. This can sometimes make the cat look sad so can also be referred to as a 'tragic facial expression'

Congenital hypothyroidism is very rare although it has been reported in most breeds of cats, including Abyssinian and domestic shorthair (moggies). Typical signs of this illness include:

- Disproportionate stunting – a kitten which is small with very short legs, a short body and a disproportionately large and broad head

- Constipation

- A goitre

- Retained baby teeth (or very delayed replacement of these by the adult teeth)

- Learning difficulties – for example difficult or impossible to litter train

- Lethargy

- Coat changes – for example a thick undercoat

- Heat seeking behaviour – hypothyroid cats may feel cold

SECTION 2 | explaining the science of hyperthyroidism

Hypothyroid cats have low blood levels of thyroid hormones which cannot be increased much by administration of TRH (a TRH stimulation test can be done as described on page 19). Hypothyroid cats often have increased blood levels of cholesterol and a mild anaemia. Hypothyroidism is not normally treated unless it is causing clinical signs such as those listed above. Affected cats can be treated with thyroid replacement hormone (L-thyroxine) to correct this condition. Congenital cases do not always make a full response to treatment and some owners elect for euthanasia in cats whose quality of life is considered to be unacceptably poor.

Congenital hypothyroidism is very rare. Typical signs include disproportionate stunting as can be seen in this kitten which was very small with short legs, a short body and a disproportionately large head. (The cat is pictured next to a 400g tin of catfood to give an indication of scale).

SECTION 2 | explaining the science of hyperthyroidism

What is the best treatment for my hyperthyroid cat?

As already discussed, all of the treatments available have advantages and disadvantages. The best person to advise you regarding your cat is your own veterinary surgeon since they know you and your cat best. The advantages and disadvantages are summarised in the table below. Often there is not a huge difference in cost between the different treatments. The cost of medical treatment is spread over the remaining years of the cat's life rather than required at the start of treatment.

Factor	Medical treatment	Surgery	Radioiodine
Is it possible to cure the condition with this treatment?	No	Yes	Yes
Are side-effects possible?	Yes	Yes	Yes
How common and how serious are the side effects?	< 20% of cats have mild and transient side-effects. < 5% of cats have serious side effects	Typically < 10% of cats suffer side-effects but these can be very serious	< 5% of cats suffer side-effects and these are usually treatable
Is there a risk of hypothyroidism?	No – the dose of treatment can be reduced	Very rare (< 5%)	Very rare (< 5%)
Is there a risk of recurrence?	Yes	Yes	Yes (much less common)
Will my cat need to stay in hospital?	Not usually	Yes, usually < 3-5 days	Yes, usually at least 1 week*
Will the treatment be available in my location?	Yes	Yes	Less common

* the duration of hospitalisation varies enormously according to the location and radiation rules in that area.

SECTION 2 | explaining the science of hyperthyroidism

Can hyperthyroid cats with chronic kidney disease still receive treatment?

Treatment of hyperthyroid cats with chronic kidney disease is complicated. As discussed earlier (pages 33-34), all treatments for hyperthyroidism have the potential to worsen kidney function. This is because all treatments of hyperthyroidism cause a reduction in blood flow to the kidneys. This has the potential to 'unmask' or reveal kidney disease that was not previously known about and to worsen pre-existing kidney disease.

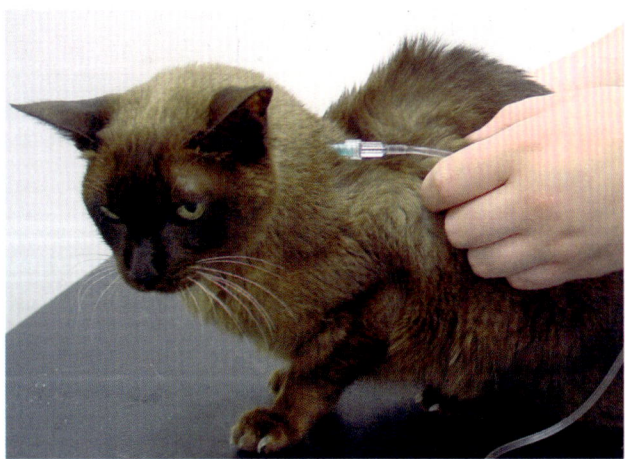

Treatment of hyperthyroid cats with kidney disease is more complicated since all treatments have the potential to worsen kidney function. Medical management of the hyperthyroidism using antithyroid drugs is usually recommended since this is a reversible treatment – the dose can be reduced or even stopped if necessary. Other treatments for kidney disease such as subcutaneous fluid therapy (shown here) can be continued.

Assessment of kidney function is complicated in a cat with hyperthyroidism (see pages 20-21). If a cat is known to have chronic kidney disease before medical treatment is started then your vet may recommend that a lower dose of medication (such as methimazole or carbimazole) is used initially and that the kidney values are monitored closely using blood tests. If any problems are seen, then the dose of treatment can be lowered or even stopped. It can be a delicate balance between treating the thyroid disease and yet not compromising kidney function.

If the kidney disease remains stable on hyperthyroid treatment, and your cat remains well, then more permanent treatments for the hyperthyroidism (such as surgery and radioiodine) can be considered. Treatment for chronic kidney disease is discussed in more detail in another Cat Professional publication 'Caring for a cat with kidney failure'. The recent treatment advances for kidney disease have been very successful in stabilising cats with this condition.

Can hyperthyroid cats with diabetes mellitus still receive treatment?

Treatment of hyperthyroid cats with diabetes mellitus is more complicated. Thyroid hormones cause insulin resistance by interfering with the way insulin (the hormone that regulates blood sugar levels) is able to work. In those cats that are diabetic before they develop hyperthyroidism, the thyroid disease can make medical control of the diabetes more difficult. Often it is necessary to stabilise the hyperthyroidism before the diabetes can, once again, be fully controlled.

SECTION 2 | explaining the science of hyperthyroidism

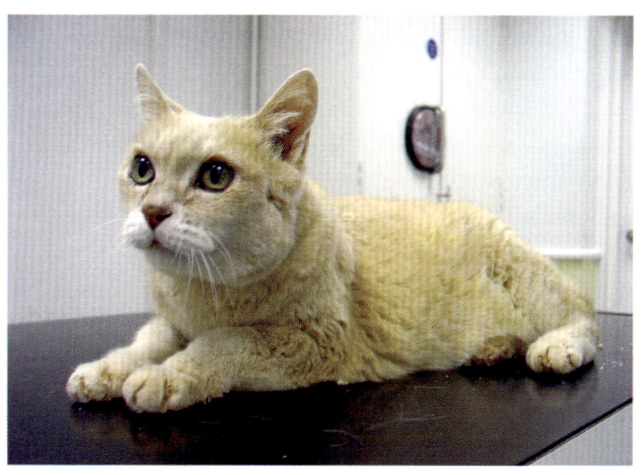

Treatment of diabetic hyperthyroid cats is more complicated. Often it is necessary to stabilise the hyperthyroidism before the diabetes can be fully controlled.

A cat whose diabetes was previously well controlled may deteriorate when hyperthyroidism develops. In some cats with both illnesses, a higher dose of insulin might be needed to stabilise blood sugar levels. However, until the thyroid disease has been brought under control, your vet may recommend that a low dose of insulin is used and that your cat's diabetes is monitored closely. This is done to avoid the problem of low blood sugar levels (hypoglycaemia) developing once the thyroid disease comes under control. Hypoglycaemia can be fatal and is much more concerning in the short-term than uncontrolled diabetes mellitus.

In a small number of hyperthyroid cats, insulin resistance caused by this condition can lead to development of diabetes mellitus.

What about cats with thyroid carcinomas?

Thyroid carcinomas are a rare cause of hyperthyroidism (approximately 1 – 2% of patients) but are much more serious. A carcinoma is a type of cancer. The abnormal thyroid tissue not only grows and enlarges causing hyperthyroidism and a goitre but also:

- Can invade healthy tissues adjacent to the thyroid. This often means that the cancer is impossible to remove surgically or that very radical surgery is required (for example removing portions of neck muscle as well as the goitre).

- Can spread to other parts of the body such as the lungs.

Some thyroid carcinomas may be manageable with antithyroid drugs (for example carbimazole or methimazole). Surgical treatment is not usually advised in these patients since it is generally not possible to remove all of the cancerous tissue, even with radical surgery. The treatment of choice is radioiodine but a much higher dose is required – typically five to ten times the dose needed

Thyroid carcinomas are best treated with a very high dose of radioiodine. This patient had a very successful response to treatment. She was cured of her thyroid disease and lived for many more years with an excellent quality of life.

SECTION 2 | explaining the science of hyperthyroidism

with 'routine' hyperthyroid cats. This poses some additional problems in terms of human health and safety since the level of radiation is much higher. Only a few locations are able to offer treatment for thyroid carcinomas – in the UK, the University of Bristol is the only place where thyroid carcinomas can be treated (see Useful websites for more information).

How can I give my cat the best quality and length of life possible?

For many cats, once stabilised, their care is not difficult, time-consuming or stressful and it is likely that they will enjoy a good quality of life for years.

Regular monitoring and vigilance for development of new problems are essential in ensuring the best care of your cat. It is important to follow your vet's recommendations regarding timing and frequency of check-ups. The precise timing of these varies from cat to cat, according to the treatment regime they are receiving and their progress on this.

> **Check-ups are especially important for cats receiving antithyroid medication. Although severe side-effects are very rare, they can be fatal if not detected and treated promptly.**

Check-ups for hyperthyroid cats receiving medical treatment

Check-ups and monitoring are especially important for cats receiving medical therapy for their hyperthyroidism. Typically these involve:

■ History and clinical examination:

– Aim of these tests: to assess the progress of the patient since starting treatment both looking for evidence suggesting that the hyperthyroidism is now controlled and also for any evidence of side-effects to treatment. For example, a racing heart rate can imply that the disease is still not under control; a healthy weight gain should be seen with successful management of the hyperthyroidism.

– Frequency of check-up required:

• It is most common for the first check-up to be timetabled around three weeks after treatment has been started. If the thyroid hormone levels are too high or too low, the treatment dose may need to be changed and a repeat check-up arranged. Repeat check-ups are usually done approximately every three weeks until the thyroid disease is stable and the thyroid hormone levels are within the reference range (known as euthyroidism).

• For those cats whose hyperthyroidism has been successfully stabilised with antithyroid drugs, check-ups are recommended after a further three, five to six, eight

SECTION 2 | explaining the science of hyperthyroidism

Weight checks are very important – success of treatment can be partly assessed by monitoring the cat's bodyweight.

to ten and 20 weeks. After this time, check-ups every three months are recommended for as long as the cat remains on antithyroid medication. Laboratory tests should also be done if there is any concern as a result of the history and/or clinical examination – for example if your vet is suspicious of anaemia (for example if your cat's gums appear very pale) then a haematology profile may be indicated to assess the numbers of red blood cells, platelets and haemoglobin content.

– Why are these check-ups important?

- A veterinary examination is the best way of detecting changes which might not be obvious at home since the care provider is seeing their cat every day. For example, weight loss commonly goes unnoticed by owners (unless it becomes quite dramatic) as it is impossible to observe a small daily amount of weight loss when you are seeing your cat every day. I have seen many cats that have lost 10-20% of their body weight since the last check-up but whose owners are unaware of any change in their condition (or even think that their cat has gained weight!). Imagine how much weight loss this would be for you and hence how serious a consequence this could be for your cat!

- A check-up every three months ensures that any problem, such as weight loss, is detected promptly and can therefore be addressed quickly.

- Three monthly check–ups maintain good contact with your vet. Good teamwork between you and your vet will lead to the best care and hence, best outcome for your cat.

- In many countries there is a legal requirement to see patients at least every six months if they are receiving prescription medicines such as antithyroid drugs.

■ Blood pressure measurement (where possible) and eye examination (to look for evidence of high blood pressure)

SECTION 2 | explaining the science of hyperthyroidism

should be done following a diagnosis of hyperthyroidism. Examination of the eyes is something that can easily be done at the general check-ups and therefore can continue to be done whenever the cat comes in for a check-up. Since a proportion of cats develop systemic hypertension after their hyperthyroidism has been treated, continued monitoring is also important following medical stabilisation.

– Aim of these tests: to identify and treat high blood pressure promptly. If left untreated, high blood pressure risks serious consequences such as permanent blindness, kidney damage and death.

– Frequency of check-up required:

- If blood pressure is normal at the initial check then I would advocate a second check within the first two months to ensure that high blood pressure is not being overlooked. If still normal at this point then I would reduce the frequency of blood pressure check-ups to a minimum of two checks per year.

- In those cats needing treatment for systemic hypertension, blood pressure needs to be checked more frequently – especially during the initial period of treatment. Once blood pressure is stable subsequent check-ups can be done less frequently. This is something that I do gradually according to the patient – for example reducing the frequency of blood pressure checks to a minimum of three to four checks per year, even if very stable.

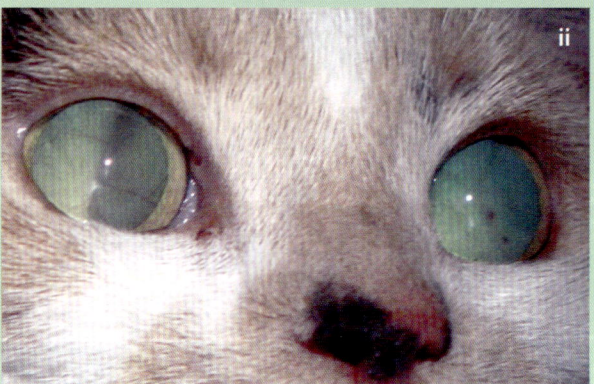

Dilation of the pupils (i) is one potential indication of blindness associated with high blood pressure as in this case. When a light is shone into the cat's eyes (ii), the pupils remain large and the retina can be seen (both of these findings are abnormal). Small areas of bleeding can also be seen in the cat's left eye – another consequence of her high blood pressure. Unfortunately the blindness was permanent in this cat.

SECTION 2 | explaining the science of hyperthyroidism

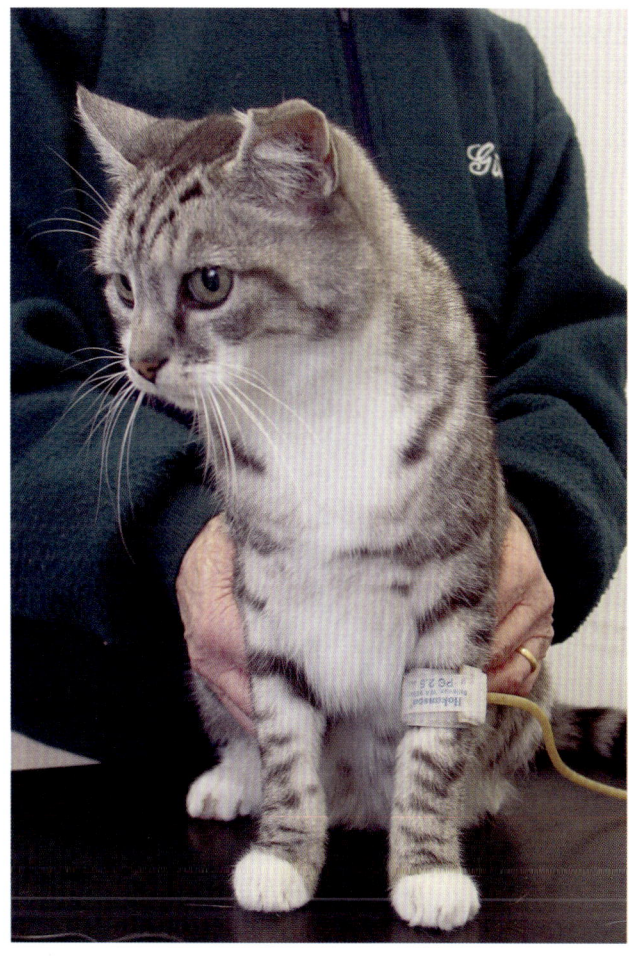

Blood pressure assessment is an important part of the check-up examination. This cat has a leg cuff on in readiness to measure his blood pressure.

– Why are such regular check-ups needed in all cats?

- A proportion of hyperthyroid cats develop systemic hypertension after their hyperthyroidism is treated and it is important to identify and treat these cats. In some of these cats, the high blood pressure is associated with chronic kidney disease. Systemic hypertension is often referred to as the 'silent killer' – it is common to show no outward signs of this condition before severe problems strike. Blood pressure checks ensure that high blood pressure is identified quickly helping to prevent development of consequences associated with this condition.

■ Repeat laboratory tests: haematology, serum biochemistry, urinalysis and total thyroxine (tT4)

– Aim of these tests:

- To check whether the thyroid disease is under control (i.e. whether or not the thyroid hormone levels are within the reference range), to assess whether there are any concurrent illnesses and to look for side-effects associated with the treatment (e.g. changes to the haematology). Most side-effects are seen within the first few months of therapy and laboratory tests are especially important during this period.

– Frequency of check-up required:

- For cats whose hyperthyroidism is still not fully controlled (thyroid hormone levels still too high), repeat tT4 assessment is usually recommended two to three weeks after any treatment dose change until euthyroidism is achieved. At these checks it is desirable, where possible, to include additional laboratory tests to check kidney function and look for potential side-effects to treatment.

- For those cats whose hyperthyroidism has been successfully stabilised with antithyroid drugs, check-ups are recommended after a further three, five to six, eight to ten and 20 weeks. After this time, check-ups every three months are recommended for as long as the cat remains on antithyroid medication. As discussed earlier, laboratory tests should also be done if there is any specific concern as a result of the history and/or clinical examination such as anaemia or weight loss.

– Why are these check-ups important?

- Laboratory tests are important to ensure that treatment is successful and to check for evidence of any side-effects. For example, it is important to look for worsening of kidney function that may necessitate a reduction in the dose of antithyroid medication. In addition, as discussed on pages 36-37, laboratory tests are needed to look for evidence of severe side-effects associated with antithyroid treatment. Although severe side-effects are very rare, these can be fatal in some cats. Prompt treatment provides the best chance of a successful outcome.

Check-ups for hyperthyroid cats that have had surgical treatment or radioiodine

Check-ups are still very important in these cats. Typically these involve:

■ History and clinical examination:

– Aim of these tests: to assess the progress of the patient since treatment was given both looking for evidence suggesting that the hyperthyroidism is now controlled and also for any evidence of side-effects related to the treatment. For example, hair loss over the ears can be an indication of hypothyroidism; an increased thirst may be an indication of chronic kidney disease.

– Frequency of check-up required:

- Cats that have had surgical treatment will usually be reassessed a few days after their surgery so that their surgical wound can be checked for any swelling or other problems. If stitches have been placed in the skin, these will normally need to stay in for 7 – 10 days.

- Cats that have suffered from post-operative hypoparathyroidism need frequent assessments (for example weekly) and careful management until their hypoparathyroidism has resolved. Dosages of calcium and vitamin D need to be carefully titrated in these cats to ensure that they are receiving the correct treatment.

SECTION 2 | explaining the science of hyperthyroidism

- Cats that have had radioiodine treatment will usually have check-ups at around one and three months following their treatment.

- In the long-term, cats that have had surgical or radioiodine treatment benefit from check-ups every three to six months. The main reason for these check-ups is to look for evidence of recurrence of hyperthyroidism and emergence of new problems such as kidney disease. A history and clinical examination helps to pick up clues of these such as weight loss.

— Why are these check-ups important?

- A veterinary examination is the best way of detecting changes which might not be obvious at home since the care provider is seeing their cat every day. For example, weight loss commonly goes unnoticed by owners (unless it becomes quite dramatic) as it is impossible to observe a small daily amount of weight loss when you are seeing your cat every day. A check-up every three to six months ensures that any problem, such as weight loss, is detected promptly and can therefore be addressed quickly.

- Three to six monthly check–ups maintain good contact with your vet. Good teamwork between you and your vet will lead to the best care and hence, best outcome for your cat.

■ Blood pressure measurement (where possible) and eye examination (to look for evidence of high blood pressure) should be done following a diagnosis of hyperthyroidism. Examination of the eyes is something that can easily be done at the general check-ups and therefore can continue to be done whenever the cat comes in for a check-up. Since a proportion of cats develop systemic hypertension after their hyperthyroidism has been treated, continued monitoring is also important following radioiodine and thyroid surgery.

— Aim of these tests: to identify and treat high blood pressure promptly. If left untreated, high blood pressure risks serious consequences such as permanent blindness, kidney damage and death.

SECTION 2 | explaining the science of hyperthyroidism

– Frequency of check-up required:

- If blood pressure is normal at the initial check then I would advocate a second check within the first two months to ensure that high blood pressure is not being overlooked. If still normal at this point then I would reduce the frequency of blood pressure check-ups to a minimum of two checks per year.

- In those cats needing treatment for systemic hypertension, blood pressure needs to be checked more frequently – especially during the initial period of treatment. Once blood pressure is stable subsequent check-ups can be done less frequently. This is something that I do gradually according to the patient – for example reducing the frequency of blood pressure checks to a minimum of three to four checks per year, even if very stable.

– Why are such regular check-ups needed in all cats?

- A proportion of hyperthyroid cats develop systemic hypertension after their hyperthyroidism is treated and it is important to identify and treat these cats. In some of these cats, the high blood pressure is associated with chronic kidney disease. Systemic hypertension is often referred to as the 'silent killer' – it is common to show no outward signs of this condition before severe problems strike. Blood pressure checks ensure that high blood pressure is identified quickly helping to prevent development of consequences associated with this condition.

■ Repeat laboratory tests: haematology, serum biochemistry, urinalysis and total thyroxine (tT4)

– Aim of these tests:

- To check whether the thyroid disease has recurred (i.e. whether or not the thyroid hormone levels are within the reference range), to assess whether there are any concurrent illnesses and to look for side-effects associated with the treatment (such as worsened kidney function).

– Frequency of check-up required:

- Check-ups are recommended at one and three months after surgery or radioiodine. Very occasionally, some hyperthyroid cats treated with radioiodine may take longer than three months to become euthyroid.

- After this period, if all remains well, check-ups are recommended every 6-12 months. Laboratory tests should also be done if there is any concern as a result of the history and/or clinical examination – for example if your cat has lost weight, a thyroid hormone test may be indicated to assess whether the hyperthyroidism has recurred.

– Why are these check-ups important?

- 'Unmasking' of kidney disease or worsening of existing kidney disease can occur following treatment for

SECTION 2 | explaining the science of hyperthyroidism

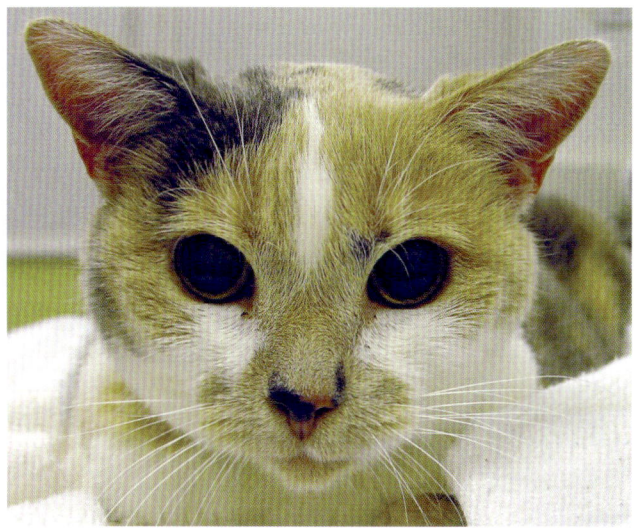

Sudden blindness, often associated with dramatic dilatation of the pupils (the black slit in the centre of the eye becomes very large and round, as in this cat), is a veterinary emergency. Systemic hypertension is the most common cause of this.

Cats should be returned for check-ups sooner if you have any concerns. Specific causes for concern include:

- Sudden deterioration or loss of vision

- Loss of appetite which persists for more than 24 hours

- Vomiting more frequently

- Severe lethargy/listlessness

- Scratching and severe itchiness of the skin (especially the head area) in cats receiving antithyroid medication

hyperthyroidism. It is important to identify this as soon as possible so that appropriate treatment can be given.

- It is important to confirm that the surgical or radioiodine treatment has been successful in treating the hyperthyroidism. In some cats, radioiodine can take several months to be fully effective.

- Hyperthyroidism can recur following surgical and radioiodine treatment. Laboratory tests help to identify any recurrence quickly so that this can be treated.

Are routine vaccinations and worming still needed in cats with hyperthyroidism?

Cats with stable and well managed hyperthyroidism still benefit from routine preventative health care such as vaccination. All illnesses can reduce a cat's ability to fight infections so they will be more vulnerable to severe illness if they contract an infection. Visits to a veterinary practice can be stressful (which can lower immunity) and risk contact with infectious agents.

As always, follow your vet's advice on what is most appropriate for your cat. For example, an indoor-only cat that has no access to hunting or fleas does not generally need to be de-wormed or treated with flea prevention products.

SECTION 2 | explaining the science of hyperthyroidism

What is the prognosis (long-term outlook) for cats with hyperthyroidism?

Overall, most hyperthyroid cats live for between two and five years following diagnosis of this condition. The best prognosis is reported in those cats treated with radioiodine. Cats that are diagnosed with hyperthyroidism at a younger age are expected to live for longer than cats that are very old at the time of diagnosis. Well controlled thyroid disease is not expected to shorten life expectancy.

The prognosis varies quite markedly in affected cats and this is related to:

- Whether the cat has other concurrent illnesses which may have a life-shortening effect. A common example would be chronic kidney disease. Cats with severe concurrent kidney disease have a reduced lifespan compared to otherwise healthy hyperthyroid cats.

- Whether the cat has severe complications associated with their thyroid disease. Although these usually improve with treatment of the thyroid condition, some can still be difficult to fully control. One example would be a cat suffering from severe heart disease – often heart medications are needed for the rest of the cat's life, even when the thyroid disease has been successfully treated.

SECTION 3 | case illustrations

Anna

Anna was one of the first patients I treated with radioiodine when I was working at the University of Bristol. She was referred with a typical history of hyperthyroidism – she had lost weight, had intermittent diarrhoea, was very hyperactive and irritable and had an insatiable appetite. She was eating several tins of catfood every day and still losing weight. Her poor owner had taken to sleeping downstairs so that she could feed Anna more frequently during the night!

Anna's hyperthyroidism was very advanced and this made her almost impossible to examine – she was very feisty! Her hyperthyroidism had caused a large goitre, a very rapid heart rate, she was very thin and her levels of total T4 were extremely high (190 nmol/l when the reference range is 20 – 45 nmol/l). She had slightly increased levels of liver enzymes but the remainder of her blood and urine tests were fine. Anna had an enlarged heart as a result of her hyperthyroidism but she was not suffering from congestive heart failure. I recommended radioiodine treatment for Anna – she had been a difficult cat to give antithyroid medications to and her owner was keen for her to have the best treatment possible. She had a single subcutaneous (under the skin) injection of iodine and stayed in our hospital for a few weeks whilst she was considered 'radioactive'. At the end of her hospitalisation period, we checked Anna's total T4 levels and found that her condition had been cured (her total T4 levels were now 23 nmol/l, within the reference range). She'd also gained a healthy amount of weight and was looking much happier.

Anna's owner sent me several pictures of Anna, before and after her treatment. In the pre-treatment picture you can appreciate how thin and anxious she looks. Just a few months later, after her radioiodine treatment, she looks a completely different cat. Not only has she gained weight, but she also has a very relaxed expression. Her owner reported that Anna was 'really very healthy and content' and she was delighted that she had improved so much. Anna continued to do very well and is a great example of how well this treatment can work.

Anna before (left) and a few months after (right) treatment with radioiodine. Before treatment she was painfully thin and very anxious. The second photo shows a contented Anna who is now a healthy weight.

SECTION 3 | case illustrations

The Wilkinson hyperthyroid cats (written by their owner, Kathy)

I know quite a bit about hyperthyroidism as a result of having had seven cats diagnosed with this condition over the last five years. No two cats have been the same in the clinical signs they've shown or in their response to treatment. Several of our cats have only been diagnosed because of a routine check – not all of them have had really obvious clinical signs. They've all been treated using antithyroid medications with thyroid surgery also done in most of the cats. In some of the cats, surgery has not been appropriate and these cats have remained on lifelong antithyroid treatment. My knowledge of this disease has helped us to diagnose the condition earlier and I hope that this has led to a better treatment outcome for my cats.

Our first cat to be diagnosed was Tiffany, a 13 year old tabby and white shorthair moggy (domestic short hair). She started to hide away under the bed, which wasn't like her at all, and seemed very weak and depressed. Our vet said that her heart was beating so fast it was difficult to count. Blood tests confirmed that she was hyperthyroid, with 'apathetic' disease. This is one of the more unusual presentations of this condition and is usually seen in cats with severe heart disease.

Tiffany was an absolute nightmare to give tablets to – she got so distressed with our attempts that it was easier for us to go to the surgery every day for three weeks and ask them to medicate her! Fortunately her operation went well and she came home three days later. Although she had a slow recovery from her surgery, she gradually improved and went back to her old self.

 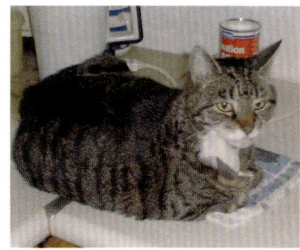

L to R: Tiffany and Tabitha.

Unfortunately about seven months later she developed another problem from which she passed away.

Having learnt a lot about hyperthyroidism through Tiffany and her illness, we soon realised that her litter sister, Tabitha, also 13 years old and tabby and white, was showing what seemed to be the textbook signs. She'd lost weight in spite of having an excellent appetite and had also become very irritable. Our vets confirmed that she too was hyperthyroid. Luckily she was much better at taking pills – especially if we hid them in a piece of meat – so we stabilised her at home before she had thyroid surgery. All went well and she made great progress following her operation. Unfortunately, about two years later, her hyperthyroidism recurred and she developed other problems. She now has systemic hypertension (and therefore can't see very well) and chronic kidney disease which means that she is not a good candidate for further surgery. We're treating her hyperthyroidism and systemic hypertension with medication and keeping a close eye on her. Tabitha was also diagnosed

SECTION 3 | case illustrations

L to R: Henry, Teddy, Nimrod.

as being diabetic not long after her initial surgery, but within about six months she self-cured – not many cats do that I am told, but she's my miracle old girl!

About a year after Tiffany and Tabitha were diagnosed, I became suspicious of signs that two of my 14 year old moggies (Henry and Teddy) were showing, and they too had blood tests for hyperthyroidism. Both cats seemed to be losing weight in spite of a very good appetite. Teddy and Henry are moggy brothers that are not related to Tiffany and Tabitha but are a similar age. Henry's T4 was within normal limits, but he was found to have a heart problem so needed treatment for this. He continued to have regular blood tests to check for hyperthyroidism, and started antithyroid medication when the levels increased. In spite of increasing doses of antithyroid drugs, his T4 levels increased and were affecting his heart. We made a decision for him to have thyroid surgery fairly quickly as he seemed to be deteriorating very rapidly. The operation went very well, and he continued to have regular blood tests and heart scans.

Henry did very well for about 18 months after his surgery but then we found that his hyperthyroidism was recurring. He had a second thyroidectomy, aged 17, as we did not want him to deteriorate and not be well enough for surgery. Unfortunately, although Henry recovered well from his thyroid surgery and his heart and kidneys remained in good condition, he developed another problem which was the cause of his death in March 2009.

Henry's brother Teddy also developed hyperthyroidism when he was 14 years old. However, he was found to have kidney problems and treating both this and the hyperthyroidism proved very difficult. It was like walking a knife's edge coping with the kidney problems and hyperthyroidism. We were able to keep him stable on antithyroid medication for about 18 months but sadly his quality of life deteriorated and eventually we asked our vet to put him to sleep.

At the beginning of 2008 Nimrod, a 12 year old male Tonkinese of mine was showing signs that I recognised from the other cats – including weight loss, vomiting and diarrhoea. He proved a difficult patient to diagnose as his total T4 was within the normal range. In spite of this, I was convinced that he was hyperthyroid and managed to persuade my vet to run a free-T4 test. I was very pleased as this confirmed my diagnosis! Nimrod had a reaction to the antithyroid treatment he was prescribed – he developed a very itchy head and neck. Fortunately we managed to stabilise him on a different treatment and he then had a thyroidectomy. His thyroid surgery was successful and his blood results are still all fine although we are monitoring him closely.

JD, one of my Mum's cats who I look after, was the next cat to develop this condition. At the time, she was nine and was found to have an enlarged thyroid gland on a routine check by our

SECTION 3 | case illustrations

vet. She too was stabilised medically before having surgery. This was successful, and on her first three month check her hormone levels were fine. However at the next three month check they were high, so we decided to stabilise her medically before having a second thyroidectomy. She's made an excellent recovery and her blood test results continue to be fine at the moment.

Bruno.

Finally, last year another of my Tonkinese (Bruno, a half brother to Nimrod) developed hyperthyroidism. He was being closely monitored for early kidney disease which had been diagnosed six months previously. A routine blood test to check his kidney function showed that he was also hyperthyroid. It came as a big shock to us as there had been no suggestion that he might be suffering from hyperthyroidism. We managed to stabilise his thyroid disease without causing any problems to his kidneys and he was able to have surgery later in the year. After his surgery, he developed an unusual complication called Horner's syndrome. This occurs when there is damage to the nerves that supply the eyes (the sympathetic nervous system). Thankfully he gradually improved and within a few weeks you couldn't tell that he had had a 'funny' eye. His kidneys have remained fine and he continues to have regular checks for these as well as for his thyroid.

I think the worst part of coping with hyperthyroidism in cats is giving the medication. It may be difficult enough to get a ten day course of antibiotics into a cat, but to face a future of once or twice daily medication is really difficult. The cost of the surgery is initially off-putting, especially when there are still regular blood checks to be done afterwards, but at least most of my cats have not needed long-term medication to keep their hyperthyroidism under control.

My choice to let my hyperthyroid cats have surgery was partly because of the difficulties associated with medicating some of my cats but also because I wanted to cure the hyperthyroidism, if at all possible. My local practice has an excellent vet who does all of the thyroid operations and this helped to reassure me about the procedure.

I would have liked to have had radioactive iodine (radioiodine) treatment for my cats but unfortunately there are often waiting lists for treatment and UK regulations mean that treated cats are usually away from home for longer than a month which has put me off. I would be happier if two of my cats could go together – the Tonkinese in particular are cats that get very lonely if they don't have company. When I've discussed hyperthyroidism with US cat friends, I've found that radioactive iodine is very popular and that a typical hospitalisation period is much shorter (usually 10-14 days).

My biggest concern, however, is worrying about why I have had so many hyperthyroid cats. I would love to know the answer so that I can avoid my younger cats suffering from this condition. I have read about all sorts of factors that have been studied as possible causes of hyperthyroidism but I am still frustrated that more is not known.

SECTION 4 | discussing your cat's health with your vet

A good relationship with your vet is vital to the care and wellbeing of your cat with hyperthyroidism. It is important therefore that you feel able to discuss all of your concerns openly. Your vet is in the best position to advise you regarding specific questions on treatment and prognosis. You should feel able to ask your vet any questions and they should be able to explain things to you clearly in a way you can understand.

If you feel that the relationship you have with your vet is not answering your concerns then you can ask to see another vet within the practice, or look for another practice. Do not feel uncomfortable if you want to do this – your vet should not mind and it is within your rights to choose the vet you feel is best able to look after your cat. It is always worthwhile asking if there is anyone in the practice who is particularly interested in cat medicine. The UK cat charity, the Feline Advisory Bureau, has a list of UK (and some overseas) vet practices that are members of the charity (see http://www.fabcats.org/owners/choosing_a_vet/practice_members1.php). Belonging to this charity is a good indication of enthusiasm and knowledge in feline medicine. A number of feline-only practices also exist and you may be fortunate in finding one of these in your area. Cat owners can also consult the American Association of Feline Practitioners website for information on finding a cat vet in the US and other countries (see http://www.catvets.com/findadoctor/findadoctor.aspx).

Veterinary surgeons specialising in feline medicine can be contacted by your vet for further advice, if needed, or referral to a specialist can be arranged.

> **A good relationship with your vet is vital to the care and wellbeing of your cat with hyperthyroidism.**

In order for your vet to be able to provide the level of care you are looking for with your cat, they will need to understand things from your perspective. For example:

- Will you be able to medicate your cat at home or is this out of the question (for example because your cat is very feisty or because you have severe arthritis in your fingers)? Will giving some medications be possible (e.g. dietary treatment) but others not possible (e.g. tablets)?

- What are your expectations for your cat? For example, would you prefer minimum intervention accepting a potentially shorter time with your cat or are you keen for your cat to have every possible treatment?

- Are there any treatments which you object to being used in your cat?

- Are finances limited in which case certain treatments may be too expensive? Your vet will be able to advise you on the likely cost of treating your cat.

Once both of you know what your expectations are then it should be possible to jointly work out a treatment plan that is appropriate for your cat.

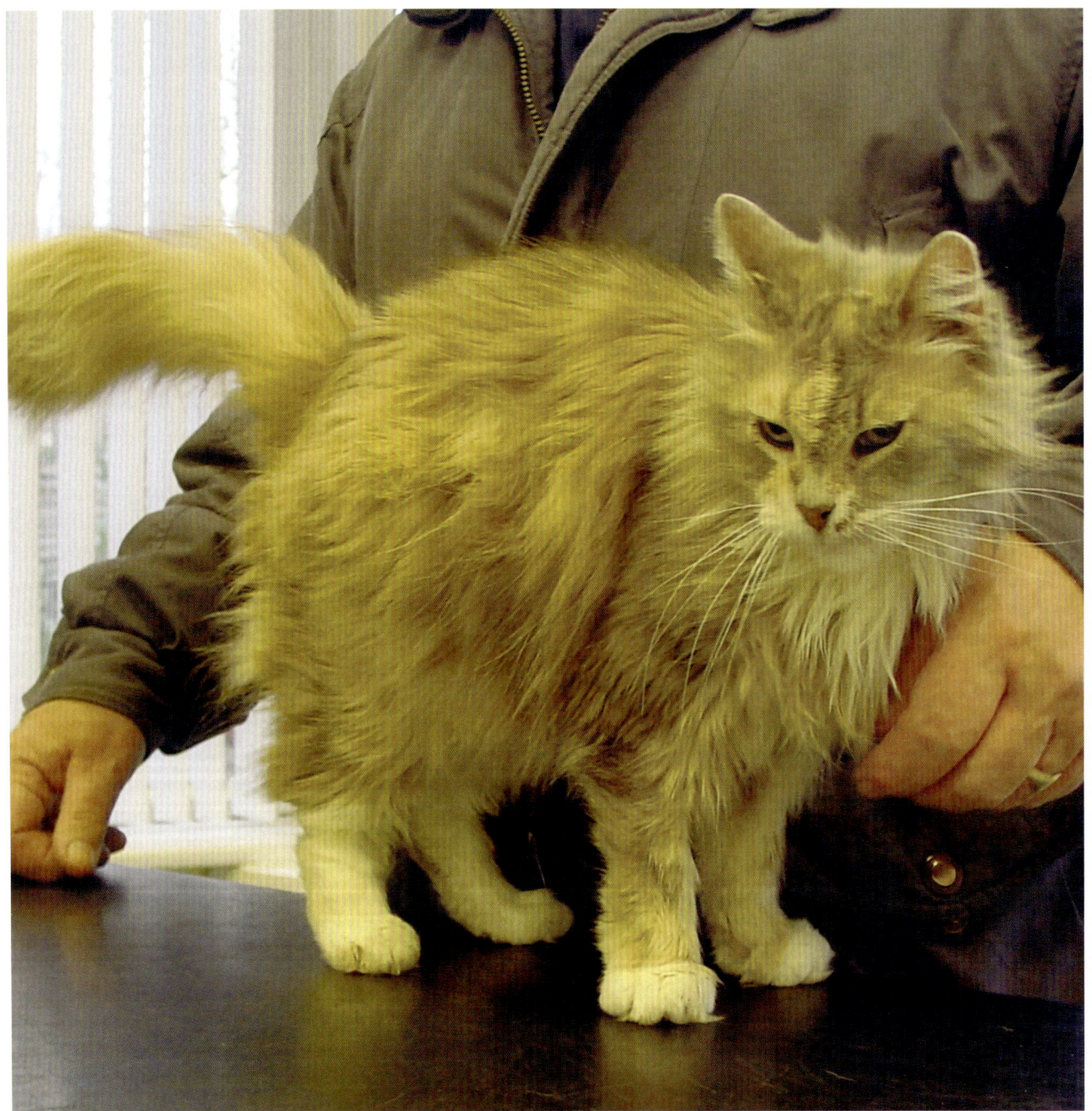

SECTION 5 | further information

The information in this section is particularly relevant to owners of cats suffering from severe disease such as hyperthyroidism which is difficult to treat because of its severity or presence of concurrent illnesses such as chronic kidney disease.

Knowing when to say 'goodbye'

How long has my cat got before he/she dies or needs to be put to sleep (euthanased)?

This is an impossible question for anyone to answer as it varies enormously from cat to cat. Most cats can live a normal quality of life for many years after a diagnosis of hyperthyroidism has been made. Sadly some die or need to be put to sleep (euthanased). This may be because of the severity of their disease or because they have other concurrent problems which are affecting them. Your vet is in the best position to advise on your own cat and its likely prognosis.

Will I know when it's time to say goodbye to my cat and let him/her go?

It is very rare for a sick cat to die painlessly in their sleep – much though most owners would wish this to happen. Death tends to be a slow and distressing process and it is far kinder to intervene and ask a vet to put your cat to sleep (euthanase it) when the time has come than let your cat suffer a prolonged and possibly painful death. It is therefore a sad inevitability that one day you are likely to have to decide that your cat needs putting to sleep.

For many owners the thought of making this decision is painful and worrying. Most owners feel that their cat should be put to sleep once their quality of life has deteriorated and there is no veterinary treatment that can help to improve this. Your vet should be able to support and guide you in making this decision – if you are at all worried then consult them for advice.

Quality of life is not easy to judge but guidelines include:

- Behaviour:

a) Is your cat still behaving in its normal way – following its usual routines and activities (e.g. spending the same amount of time grooming)? Is your cat interacting with you as normal?

b) OR, has your cat become withdrawn and quiet, not interested in going outside (if normally allowed out) or in interacting with you and other animals in the home?

- Appetite:

a) Is your cat still interested in food?

b) OR, has their appetite disappeared and getting them to eat has become a struggle?

- Toileting behaviour:

a) Is your cat still passing urine and faeces in the litter tray (or outside in the garden) as is normal for them?

SECTION 5 | further information

b) OR, has your cat started to pass urine and faeces in other places (such as on their bed or on your carpets and flooring)?

- Vocalisation:

a) Is your cat as chatty as normal?

b) OR, has there been a change in the amount of vocalisation (increase or decrease) or the sound that your cat makes when miaowing?

- Pain or distress:

a) Does your cat seem happy and comfortable?

b) OR, have you seen any sign of pain or discomfort – for example signs of fear or aggression when being handled or sitting in the same place for hours with a glazed expression?

- Signs of illness:

a) Is your cat free of signs of illness?

b) OR, is it suffering from signs of illness such as vomiting, weight loss or constipation?

If you answer b) to any of the above questions then you should consult your vet for advice on whether there are any treatments that can help your cat to regain its quality of life. If there are, you need to consider whether to give these treatments a try before making any final decisions.

What does euthanasia involve?

For most veterinary surgeons, euthanasia involves giving an overdose injection of a barbiturate anaesthetic agent intravenously, usually into a vein in the front leg. Once the injection is started, the cat will lose consciousness within a few seconds and the heart should stop within a few minutes. Occasionally, the veins of the front leg can be very fragile and difficult to access so alternative injection sites need to be used – these include the kidneys and the liver. In any case, the process should be quick and painless.

Although the majority of cats are put to sleep at a veterinary practice, most vets will be happy to come to an owner's home to do this, if desired.

What happens to my cat's body after they die or are euthanased (put to sleep)?

In general the options will be:

- Burying your cat's body at home.

- Asking your vet to arrange cremation of your cat's body. If desired, you can ask for an individual cremation to be performed and for the ashes to be returned to you.

Your vet will be able to discuss these options with you. It is worthwhile considering how you would like your cat to be put to sleep (should the need arise) and what you would like to

SECTION 5 | further information

happen to their body while your cat is still well. This will save you the added distress of these decisions when your cat dies.

How to cope with losing your cat

Is there support available for me in my grief?
Losing a beloved cat is always going to be a traumatic and distressing experience and you are likely to go through several acknowledged stages of grief. These include denial, anger, guilt, hopelessness/depression and finally acceptance. Most people experience at least two of these stages. Carers of cats with terminal illnesses may start to go through this process as soon as the diagnosis is made. Where this is the case, a further stage of grief – 'bargaining' – may also be experienced where an owner is keen for their cat to live to a certain point (for example, please let them live through Christmas so we can have this time together).

Hopefully you will have friends and family that will be able to provide some support to you throughout this period. If you don't, then consider talking to the vets or nurses at your veterinary practice, your doctor or a priest – all of whom should be able to offer support. There may be local support groups available (your veterinary practice should know about these) and there is also a UK helpline available for dedicated pet bereavement counselling, the Pet Bereavement Support Service (PBSS): 0800 096 6606 open from 8.30am to 8.30pm daily. All calls are free and confidential. The PBSS also offers an e-mail support service: pbssmail@bluecross.org.uk

SECTION 5 | further information

More information on this service is available on: http://www.bluecross.org.uk/web/site/AboutUs/PetBereavement/ContactingPBSS.asp

In North America, a helpful service to consult is http://www.untilwemeetagain.ca/pages/services/support.php

What about my other cat/s – are they likely to grieve?

Yes this is possible. As with people, cats can show grief at the loss of a companion. The behaviour of a cat following the loss of a house-mate is very variable and unpredictable. Some cats seem completely unaffected by the loss, some appear happier once they are on their own whilst others may show signs of grief such as sleeping less, not eating, appearing to look for their lost companion and vocalising more or losing all interest in life.

This process can affect cats (and other animals) for up to a year following their loss. In most cases, signs of grief will disappear within six months. You can help affected cats in the following ways:

- Where possible, it is advisable to keep routines in the home the same.

- If your cat has lost its appetite then try hand-feeding food that has been slightly warmed (to just below body temperature). Consult your vet if your cat has not eaten for three or more days. A complete loss of appetite can cause a potentially fatal liver disease called hepatic lipidosis.

- Provide social interaction for your cat by spending more time with them, grooming them, talking to them and playing with them. Try to keep the interaction low key and avoid intense handling and cuddling which could appear restrictive from a feline point of view.

- Don't immediately get a new cat. Although some cats will crave the company of a new companion, the majority of cats will be more upset and distressed if a new cat is introduced too soon. Many cats prefer to be in single cat households and it is impossible to predict what they will feel about a newcomer. So, if your cat seems happy after the loss of a house-mate I would not recommend getting another cat. If, on the other hand, you are keen to expand the home or feel that your cat is 'lonely' then I would advise waiting for at least a couple of months before considering introducing a new cat. If a new cat does move in it will need to bring with it a new supply of resources (food, water, resting places and toileting areas) which are placed in separate locations in the household from those resources that are currently being used by the resident cat.

More information on feline bereavement is available on the FAB website: http://www.fabcats.org/owners/euthanasia/bereavement.html. The FAB also has advice on introducing a new cat which could be helpful once a decision has been made to get another cat: http://www.fabcats.org/behaviour/introducing/index.php

Useful websites

Several websites have been mentioned in this publication and you might find these interesting to look at:

General cat advice
The Feline Advisory Bureau (FAB)
http://www.fabcats.org
The Blue Cross
http://www.bluecross.org.uk/web/site/home/home.asp
Cats Protection
http://www.cats.org.uk/
The Royal Society for the Prevention of Cruelty to Animals
http://www.rspca.org.uk/
The Cat Group
http://www.fabcats.org/cat_group/index.html
American Association of Feline Practitioners
http://www.catvets.com/

Choosing a veterinary practice
The Feline Advisory Bureau
http://www.fabcats.org/owners/choosing_a_vet/practice_members1.php
American Association of Feline Practitioners (AAFP)
http://www.catvets.com/findadoctor/findadoctor.aspx

General information on hyperthyroidism
FAB factsheet
http://www.fabcats.org/owners/hyperthyroidism/index.php
AAFP factsheet
http://www.catvets.com/healthtopics/edical%5Fconditions/?Id=212

Winn Feline Health
http://www.winnfelinehealth.org/Pages/Feline_Hyperthyroidism_Web.pdf
Information from Washington State University
http://www.vetmed.wsu.edu/ClientED/hyperthyroidism.aspx
Information from Dechra Veterinary Products
http://www.hyperthyroidcat.co.uk/
Information from Pet Education
http://www.peteducation.com/article.cfm?c=1+2130&aid=218
Information from Dr Mark Peterson and Hypurrcat
http://www.hypurrcat.com/index2.html

An excellent video on how to give a pill or capsule to a cat
http://partnersah.vet.cornell.edu/pet/fhc/pill_or_capsule

Bereavement support
Information from The Blue Cross
http://www.bluecross.org.uk/web/site/AboutUs/PetBereavement/PBSSIntro.asp
Information from the Feline Advisory Bureau
http://www.fabcats.org/owners/euthanasia/bereavement.html

Introducing a new cat to the home
Information from the Feline Advisory Bureau
http://www.fabcats.org/behaviour/introducing/index.php
The British Columbia Society for Prevention of Cruelty to Animals (BCSPCA)
http://www.spca.bc.ca/AnimalBehaviour/cattocatintro.asp
The Indoor cat initiative – making your home environment as stimulating as possible for your cat
http://www.vet.ohio-state.edu/indoorcat.htm

Useful websites

BCSPCA Cat Welfare information
http://www.spca.bc.ca/hideperchgo/

Information on legal prescription of veterinary drugs in the UK
http://www.noahcompendium.co.uk/Compendium/Overview/-45043.html

Information on location of radioiodine treatment facilities in the UK:
University of Bristol Feline Centre
http://www.langfordvets.co.uk/feline_medicine.htm
Animal Health Trust, Newmarket
http://www.aht.org.uk/sa_medicine.html
Royal Veterinary College, London
http://www.rvc.ac.uk/QMH/Specialities/InternalMedicine.cfm
Barton Veterinary Hospital, Canterbury
http://www.barton-vets.co.uk/referrals_feline.html
University of Glasgow
http://www.gla.ac.uk/faculties/vet/smallanimalhospital/ourservices/internalmedicine/radioiodineunit/
Bishopton Veterinary Group, North Yorkshire
http://www.bishoptonvets.co.uk/small-and-domestic-animals.html
and http://www.bishoptonvets.co.uk/factsheets.html
The University of Edinburgh Feline Clinic is planning to open a treatment facility in 2010.
http://www.vet.ed.ac.uk/cliniclaserv/HfSA/FelineMedicine.htm

Information on location of radioiodine treatment facilities in North America
A directory containing many of the treatment facilities in North America, according to their location can be found on
http://www.VeterinaryPartner.com/Content.plx?P=A&A=508&S=2&EVetID=0
Northwest Nuclear Medicine, Canada
http://www.iodinecafe.com
Thyrocat treatment centres in Albany, NY, Danbury, CT, Long Island, NY, Westchester, NY, and Rochester, NY
http://thyrocat.com/inside/about.html
Radiocat Clinics, in Phoenix, AZ; Los Angeles, CA; San Mateo, CA; Middletown, CT; Wilmington, DE; Estero, FL; Atlanta, GA; Arlington Heights, IL; Indianapolis, IN; Baltimore, MD; Wakefield, MA; White Plains, NY; Pittsburgh, PA; Greenville, SC and Springfield, VA
http://www.radiocat.com/index.html

Information on location of radioiodine treatment facilities in Australia:
New South Wales
Double Bay Veterinary Clinic
http://www.doublebayvet.com.au/index.htm
Gladesville Veterinary Hospital
http://www.gladesvillevet.com.au/
University Veterinary Centre, Sydney
http://www.vetsci.usyd.edu.au/veterinary_services/sydney/referrals/medicine.shtml

Victoria
University of Melbourne
http://www.vch.unimelb.edu.au/group.php?groupID=524
Mt Evelyn Veterinary Clinic – no website. Telephone: 03 9736 3088
Seaford Veterinary Clinic – no website. Telephone: 03 9785 2611

Useful websites

Queensland
Chermside Veterinary Hospital – no website. Telephone: 07 3350 1333

South Australia
Adelaide Veterinary Specialist Centre
http://www.vetreferrals.com.au/iodine.html

Australian Capital Territory
Canberra Veterinary Hospital
http://www.canberravet.com.au/home/index.cfm

Information on location of radioiodine treatment facilities in New Zealand:
North Island
Auckland:
Veterinary Specialist Group
http://www.vsg.co.nz/
Lynfield Vet Clinic
http://www.vetsforpets.co.nz/content/view/18/113/

Hamilton:
The Pet Practice
http://www.petpractice.co.nz/
Chartwell Vet Hospital – no website. Telephone: 07 855 9072

New Plymouth:
New Plymouth District Vet Group
http://www.npvet.co.nz/npvet/

Wellington:
Central Vet Hospital Ltd – Wellington
http://www.cenvet.co.nz/
Wadestown Vet Clinic – no website. Telephone: 04 472 2012

South Island
Christchurch:
McMaster and Heap Vet Practice
http://www.mcmasterheap.co.nz/mcmasterheap/
St Albans Vet Practice – no website. Telephone: 03 355 6747
The Straven Road Vet Centre
http://www.veterinarycentre.co.nz/index.php
Hornby Vet Centre
http://www.hornbyvet.co.nz/index.html
Rolleston Vet Services – no website. Telephone: 03 347 9682
Northlands Animal Care Hospital – no website.
Telephone: 03 352 4335

Dunedin:
St Kilda Vet Centre – no website. Telephone: 03 455 2042

Please note, these may not be complete lists – your local vet should be able to tell you where the closest radioiodine facility is.

Glossary of terms used by vets

Term	Definition
Abscess	A pocket of infection, often containing a foul smelling purulent liquid (pus). One of the most common causes of an abscess is an infected wound resulting from a cat bite.
Acute kidney disease	Also referred to as acute renal failure (ARF). Sudden loss of kidney function which can be caused by one or more of the following: ■ Reduced blood supply to the kidneys (so called pre-renal ARF). Causes include heart failure and dehydration. ■ Damage to the kidneys themselves (renal or intrinsic ARF). Causes include poisoning e.g. antifreeze (ethylene glycol), eating lilies. ■ Failure of urine excretion due to urethral obstruction or rupture of the bladder. This is called post-renal ARF. Although many causes of ARF are fully treatable (and the kidney damage can be reversed), if severe and untreated, ARF can progress to permanent chronic kidney disease.
Anaesthesia	Providing a state of unconsciousness, muscle relaxation and loss of pain sensation using certain drugs (usually a combination of intravenously and by gas inhalation).
Anaemia	A reduction in the numbers of red blood cells in the circulation. Red blood cells (also known as erythrocytes) carry oxygen to the tissues of the body so anaemic cats will often be weak and listless. Anaemias are subdivided into: ■ Regenerative anaemias: ones in which the bone marrow (which manufactures red blood cells) is responding to the anaemia and trying to correct this ■ Non-regenerative anaemias: ones in which the bone marrow response (ability to produce more new erythrocytes) is insufficient or absent
Apathetic (hyperthyroidism)	Cats showing depression, lethargy and reduced appetite are often referred to as 'apathetic' hyperthyroid cases. Some of these cats are even overweight rather than thin. Apathetic means that the cat appears indifferent, showing no emotion or animation. Most apathetic hyperthyroid cats are suffering from severe heart abnormalities associated with their hyperthyroidism.

Glossary of terms used by vets

Term	Definition
Antithyroid (medication)	Drug/s directed against the thyroid gland. Antithyroid medications (such as carbimazole and methimazole) block production of the thyroid hormones T3 and T4 by the thyroid gland.
Ascites	Accumulation of fluid in the abdominal cavity (the space around all of the abdominal organs).
Azotaemia	Accumulation of protein breakdown products such as urea and creatinine in the blood. Measurement of urea and creatinine levels is used to diagnose kidney disease and dehydration.
Bilateral (thyroid)	Involving both sides.
Biochemistry	Refers to blood tests of organ function (e.g. urea and creatinine), blood salt levels and protein levels.
Biopsy	Collection and laboratory analysis of a sample of tissue e.g. thyroid biopsy.
Calcaemia	Referring to levels of calcium in the blood stream e.g. hypocalcaemia refers to sub-normal calcium levels.
Cancer	Illness caused by abnormal and uncontrolled growth of cells (sometimes referred to as persistent purposeless proliferation). Cancerous growths are malignant meaning that they not only grow where they originally start, but also can invade adjacent tissues and spread (metastasise) to other parts of the body. Common sites for metastasis include the lungs and liver. Left untreated, most cancers will ultimately cause the death of the cat.
Carcinoma	Malignant, cancerous growth of tissues such as the thyroid gland, skin or bowel.
Chronic kidney disease	Inadequate kidney function which has been present for at least 2 weeks. This is considered to be a progressive condition – it will get worse with time – although the speed of progression is variable.
Clinical examination	Examination of body systems by a veterinary surgeon or nurse. Typically this includes listening to the chest, opening the mouth and feeling the tummy.

Glossary of terms used by vets

Term	Definition
Clinical signs	The term used to describe what we would call our 'symptoms' if we were the cat e.g. sickness, loss of appetite.
Concurrent	Occurring at the same time. For example, chronic kidney disease is a common concurrent illness in cats suffering from hyperthyroidism.
Congenital	Congenital means present from birth.
Congestive heart failure	This describes the situation present when the heart is no longer able to pump effectively. Affected cats commonly suffer from breathing difficulties associated with pulmonary oedema or pleural effusion. Ascites can also be seen in cats with congestive heart failure.
Cystitis	Inflammation of the urinary bladder (where urine is stored before urination). One cause would be a bacterial infection of the urine.
Cystocentesis	Technique of urine collection using a needle and syringe. The needle is passed through the skin and into the bladder from which urine is collected.
Diabetes mellitus	Also referred to as 'sugar diabetes'. Cats with this condition are unable to regulate their blood sugar levels due to a lack of insulin (a hormone that helps control blood glucose levels) or insulin resistance (interference with the way that insulin works). Insulin is produced by the pancreas and facilitates absorption of glucose into the cells of the body. Affected cats have high blood sugar levels and common clinical signs are an increased thirst, increased amount of urine produced and weight loss in spite of a good or even increased appetite. Treatment of diabetes usually involves changes to the diet and, in many cases, injections of insulin. Hyperthyroidism can cause insulin resistance and it is not unusual to see both illnesses in the same cat.
Ectopic	Occurring in an abnormal or unusual location. For example ectopic thyroid tissue can be present under the base of the tongue or in the chest cavity.
Erythrocyte	Red blood cell. These are the cells that carry oxygen in the circulation. A lack of red blood cells is called anaemia.

Glossary of terms used by vets

Term	Definition
Erythrocytosis	This term describes the situation when there are increased numbers of red blood cells present in the circulation. Causes include dehydration, certain medical disorders (including hyperthyroidism) and bone marrow disorders.
Euthanased	The process of euthanasia (see below).
Euthanasia	Also referred to as 'putting to sleep' this is the term used when a vet ends a cat's life. This is usually done by giving an overdose of barbiturate anaesthetic into a vein – the cat dies within seconds of the injection being given.
Euthyroid, euthyroidism	Having normal blood levels of thyroid hormones. Presence of other illnesses (such as chronic kidney disease) can reduce the blood levels of total T4 and in some cats this can reduce the T4 levels into the reference range (i.e. giving a falsely normal result). This phenomenon is known as 'sick euthyroid' and defines the situation where other illnesses suppress the levels of thyroid hormones.
Goitre	An enlarged thyroid gland which can be felt through the skin. In some cases, the goitre is so large that it can be seen.
Haematology	Laboratory test assessing the blood count, numbers and types of white blood cells and platelets.
History	This is the process by which your vet gathers information on your cat and all of its problems (clinical signs).
Hyper-	Increased e.g. hyperkalaemia, hypercalcaemia: increased blood potassium levels, increased blood calcium levels.
Hyperthyroidism	Also referred to as thyrotoxicosis. This is the veterinary term used to describe an illness resulting from having excessively high blood levels of thyroid hormones. The thyroid hormones are required in healthy cats for many functions including normal growth and development. Excessive blood levels of thyroid hormones (such as is the case with hyperthyroidism) are damaging to the body and ultimately this is a fatal illness if not treated.

Glossary of terms used by vets

Term	Definition
Hypo-	Reduced e.g. hypokalaemia: low levels of potassium in the blood; hypotension: low blood pressure.
Hypocalcaemia	Low blood calcium levels. Hypocalcaemia is a potential complication associated with thyroid surgery and it can be associated with very severe, even fatal consequences.
Hypoparathyroidism	Under-functioning of the parathyroid gland which causes reduced production of parathyroid hormones. Parathyroid hormones are needed for normal control of blood calcium levels. Hypoparathyroidism is a potential complication of thyroid surgery and can cause severe hypocalcaemia.
Hypothyroidism	Under-functioning of the thyroid gland which causes reduced production of thyroid hormones. Thyroid hormones are needed for normal control of metabolic processes in the body. Hypothyroidism can occur as a congenital disease but is most common following treatment for hyperthyroidism.
Inflammation	A response of injured or damaged cells which helps to wall off the problem, eliminate infectious substances (for example) and restore healthy tissue. The classic signs of inflammation are: ■ Heat ■ Pain ■ Redness ■ Swelling ■ Loss of function
Inflammatory	Pertaining to inflammation.
Kidney disease	See acute and chronic kidney disease. In cats with hyperthyroidism, concurrent chronic kidney disease is common. It is also common for chronic kidney disease to develop or be 'unmasked' once the thyroid disease is treated.

Glossary of terms used by vets

Term	Definition
Laryngeal paralysis	An inability to fully open the larynx when breathing, caused by damage to the recurrent laryngeal nerve. Laryngeal paralysis is a rare complication of hyperthyroidism and can also be caused by thyroid surgery. Affected cats can suffer from an altered voice, breathing difficulties, noisy breathing and a cough. In severe cases, surgery may be required to treat the laryngeal paralysis. This is a very rare potential complication of thyroid surgery.
Oedema	The accumulation of excessive amounts of watery fluid in the cells or spaces between the cells.
Parathyroid	These small glands are located very close to the thyroid tissue and help to control blood levels of calcium. Two pairs of parathyroid gland are present in each cat – one pair lying outside the thyroid gland and the other pair lying inside the capsule that surrounds the thyroid. If these delicate structures are damaged or removed during thyroid surgery, affected cats can suffer from hypocalcaemia (low blood calcium levels) which can be fatal if not treated. This condition is called hypoparathyroidism.
Pathologist	A specialist in pathology who is able to diagnose the cause and/or type of disease by examining biopsy samples.
Pathology	The study of disease.
Pleural effusion	Accumulation of fluid in the chest space around the lungs.
Polydipsia	An increased thirst.
Polyphagia	An increased appetite.
Polyuria	Increased volume of urine produced (usually noticed as the cat is passing normal volumes of urine more frequently).
Prognosis	A forecast of the likely long-term outlook for a cat with a given condition/s.

Glossary of terms used by vets

Term	Definition
Pulmonary oedema	The accumulation of excessive amounts of watery fluid in the cells or spaces between the cells of the lungs. This is a common consequence of congestive heart failure in cats. Affected cats often suffer from breathlessness and are very lethargic.
Radiograph/s	X-ray/s.
Radioiodine	A form of radiotherapy that is able to treat abnormal thyroid tissue. Radioiodine contains a very small dose of radioactive iodine (^{131}I) which is given orally or by injection. Iodine is used by the thyroid gland to produce thyroid hormones. The radioactivity is able to destroy the abnormal thyroid tissue, shrinking the goitre and reducing the amount of thyroid hormones produced.
Recurrent laryngeal nerve	This is one of the nerves that supplies the larynx (voice box). Temporary or permanent damage can occur during surgery and is called laryngeal paralysis (paralysis of the larynx).
Refractometer/s	Instrument/s that can measure the concentration of urine (urine specific gravity, USG).
Scintigraphy	This technique is also referred to as a technetium scan, isotope scan or radionuclide imaging. It described the use of radioactive substances to make an image of tissues. Thyroid scintigraphy can be used to locate abnormal thyroid tissue and is particularly helpful in cats with ectopic thyroid disease.
Sedation	Providing a state of calm and muscle relaxation using drugs. The cat is still conscious but, depending on the drugs used, may appear quite sleepy.
Stricture/s	The medical term for an abnormal narrowing of a tube such as the oesophagus (food pipe). Causes of strictures include tumours and inflammation.
Sympathetic nervous system	Nerves involved in this part of the nervous system pass close to the thyroid glands and can be damaged during surgery. Affected cats can develop temporary or permanent Horner's syndrome. This is recognised as a droopy upper eyelid, smaller pupil, a sunken eye (ptosis) and protrusion of the third eyelid (sometimes referred to as the Haws or nictitating membrane). This is a very rare potential complication of thyroid surgery and is usually temporary although it may take weeks or months to resolve.

Glossary of terms used by vets

Term	Definition
Systemic hypertension	An increase in the blood pressure of the systemic blood supply (the blood supply to all of the body except the lungs).
T3	One of the thyroid hormones. Its full name is triiodothyronine.
T4	One of the thyroid hormones. Its full name is thyroxine.
Thyroid	The thyroid gland is normally located in the cat's neck, just below the larynx (voice box). The thyroid gland is made up of two lobes – one on each side of the body. The thyroid gland produces thyroid hormones (T3 and T4) which are needed to regulate metabolic processes in the body.
Thyroidectomy	Surgical removal of all or part of the thyroid gland.
Transdermal (medication)	Transdermal medication comes as a skin cream which is usually applied to the inside of the cat's ear (a hairless area). The medication is absorbed through the skin and into the blood stream. Transdermal antithyroid medications can take longer to be effective than the oral form. Transdermal medications are controversial – there is much less evidence to demonstrate their effectiveness. The skin normally forms a barrier to stop substances from entering the body so this might not always be a good way of delivering a drug to the blood stream. There are no licensed transdermal antithyroid medications available in the UK.
Trauma	Injury or wound.
Unilateral (thyroid)	Involving one side.
Urethra	The tube which carries urine from the bladder to the outside of the body.
Urethral obstruction	This is the medical term for a 'blocked cat'. A blockage in the urethra prevents the cat from being able to pass urine. This is an emergency condition since it can be fatal if left untreated.
Urinalysis	Laboratory analysis of a urine sample e.g. concentration, number of cells, acidity, protein levels.

Converting SI units to Conventional units and vice versa

Parameter	To convert Conventional to SI multiply by...	To convert SI to Conventional multiply by...
Albumin	10	0.1
Alanine aminotransferase (ALT)	1	1
Alkaline phosphatase (ALP)	1	1
Bicarbonate	1	1
Calcium	0.25	4
Cholesterol	0.0259	38.61
Creatinine	88.4	0.0113
Free T4 (fT4) by equilibrium dialysis	12.9	0.0775
Glucose	0.0555	18.02
Haemoglobin (Hb)	10	0.1
Packed cell volume (PCV) or haematocrit	0.01	100
Phosphate	0.323	3.1
Potassium	1	1
Sodium	1	1
Total protein	10	0.1
Total Thyroxine (tT4)	12.9	0.0775
Urea	0.357	2.8